DISCOVERING ART

The Life, Times and Work of the World's Greatest Artists

ILLUMINATED MANUSCRIPTS

D. M. GILL

BROCKHAMPTON PRESS

For MG
Now and Always

Publishers Note:
The reproduction of some of the manuscripts in this book is occasionally compromised
by the age of the works or transparencies, many of which are originals and cannot be replaced.
We have included them in order to provide a representative selection of illustrative reference.

First published in Great Britain by Brockhampton Press,
a member of the Hodder Headline Group,
20 Bloomsbury Street, London WC1B 3QA

ISBN 1 86019 115 0

Produced by Flame Tree Publishing,
The Long House, Antrobus Road, Chiswick, London W4 HY
for Brockhampton Press
A Wells/McCreeth/Sullivan Production

Pictures printed courtesy of the Visual Arts Library, London, The Bridgeman Art Library, London
and Edimedia, Paris,

Printed and bound by Oriental Press, Dubai

CONTENTS

Da Costa Book of Hours, Simon Bening,
Flanders, *c.* 1515 (New York, Pierpont
Morgan Library): Boating.
This calendar page for May is an idyllic
scene of young people out on the river
on a fine spring day. Branches of may
decorate their boat, and they have a
musical accompaniment.

SHORT CHRONOLOGY

AD 409	End of Roman rule in Britain
563	St Columba founds monastery on Iona
597	St Augustine arrives in Kent, sent by Pope Gregory the Great
	St Augustine's Abbey in Canterbury founded – oldest in England
635	St Aidan, sent from Iona, founds monastery at Lindisfarne
c.650	*Book of Durrow*
664	*Synod of Whitby*
674-681	Wearmouth and Jarrow monasteries founded by Benedict Biscop
687	St Cuthbert, Prior of Lindisfarne, dies
c.698	*Lindisfarne Gospels*
698	Monastery of Echternach founded; *Echternach Gospel Book*
700	*Durham Gospel Book*
731	Venerable Bede completes his *Ecclesiastical History,* writing at Wearmouth and Jarrow
735	Death of Venerable Bede
793-5	Viking raids on Lindisfarne, Jarrow and Iona
c.790	*Hereford Cathedral Gospel Book; Lichfield Gospel Book*
c.800	*Book of Kells*
800	Charlemagne crowned Emperor in Rome
1006	Lindisfarne burnt by Vikings
1066	Battle of Hastings
1096	First Crusade
1170	Thomas à Becket murdered in Canterbury Cathedral
1215	*Magna Carta*
1291	Sixth (and last) Crusade
1346	Battle of Crécy
1347–8	Black Death
1415	Battle of Agincourt
1450	*Gutenberg Bible* printed in Mainz
1453	Fall of Constantinople to the Ottoman Turks
1476	Printing introduced to England by William Caxton
1483	Martin Luther born
1492	Columbus discovers America
1521	*Diet of Worms*
1534	Luther's German translation of the Bible completed

Book of Hours of Catherine of Cleves, Master of Catherine of Cleves, *c.* 1440 (New York, Pierpont Morgan Library): Hell.
This truly terrifying depiction of the gates of Hell illustrates the Office of the Dead. Two demons gape, one displaying the eternal fires within, where other demons torture the damned, and another a part of a brooding, ominously dark edifice. Even the border decoration is sombre in tone.

CHAPTER 1

Early Middle Ages

Illuminated manuscripts were made by hand in Europe during the whole of the Middle Ages, for 900 years from the dying days of the Roman Empire to the high Renaissance; from the birth of Christianity in Europe to the birth of the printing press in the mid-fifteenth century.

Overleaf:
Franciscan calendar, late 15th cent.
(Lyon, Bibliothèque Municipale):
Bakery.
This closely observed and detailed picture of a late fifteenth-century bakery comes from a calendar showing saints' days – a name could be assigned to every day of the year. The village bakery was often a communal building, where many grades of bread would be baked.

Britain was at the very edge of the known world when the first illuminated manuscripts were made there; 900 years later explo-ration of the New World was well under way, and the old religious certainties had been swept away in the turmoil of the Reformation and Counter-Reformation. The introduction of the printed book had an impact that was almost equal to the inventions many centuries later of radio and television. It allowed the rapid spread of new ideas to all educated men, and hastened the onward march of literacy and education for all.

A thousand years ago books were written in Latin and would only have been found in a monastery. Monks themselves spent long hours in their manufacture. A monk working at the monastery of Jarrow, in north-east England, in the seventh century might have been able to complete a text in two to three months, depending of course on the size and complexity of the task. He would have had other duties to attend to at the same time, and probably would have been under no pressure to work especially fast at his writing; in fact the really big projects such as the very big Bibles or Gospel Books might well have taken years to complete and were unlikely to have been the work of only one man. However, a professional scribe working in the fifteenth century would have been paid by the item and it was very much in his interests to work fast. There exist manuscripts in which the scribe has made a note of how long the work took him; a moderate text might only take a matter of days. Illustrations might have been accomplished at the rate of two or three a day.

Many of the manuscripts written for day-to-day use in the monastery, perhaps practical handbooks or Bibles for use in the dortoir, were not decorated. The greatest Bibles and Gospel Books, however, were elaborately adorned. The main reason for this must surely have been to exalt the mystery and complexity of the Word of God with the beauty, the labour and the time given to the manuscript. In addition, however, the bright colours and the elaborately decorated initial letters on a page would have been very eye-catching, and must have helped the reader find his place in the book. In some cases, the initial letter at the start of a book or chapter would occupy most or even all of the page. Bibles were not in those days divided into the chapters and verses with which we are familiar today, so another means of finding one's place was necessary. Pictures also helped to explain the text, and provided a way to fix an image in one's head. In those early days, gold as a decoration was rare.

By about the eleventh century, more and more new texts were being written, and it was becoming harder for monks, working alone, to keep up to date. Secular scribes and illustrators, often itinerant, were increasingly employed to help with the work. The medieval artist was not a man to whom the idea of self-expression or individual genius was important. He would have taken a commission and fulfilled it exactly as he was instructed, copying from an exemplar or colouring in outlines prepared for him, using colours already chosen by the designer of the book. In the twelfth century the early universities in such European cities as Paris and Bologna were filled with students, for the first time independent of the monasteries, and all requiring textbooks. More and more people wanted to own books for themselves. By about 1200 secular workshops were producing and decorating manuscripts for sale and providing a marketplace for second-hand books, too.

Life in the Middle Ages marched to a different rhythm from that which rules our life today. Medieval country people would have worked during the hours of daylight and any divisions of time would have been marked by the local monastery bell. The Venerable Bede, the monk of Jarrow in Northumbria who died there in about 735, was responsible for promoting the idea of a Christian year, *annus domini*, for dating purposes – and over the following centuries the idea was taken up all over Europe. Other places had other ways of dating documents and of reckoning the year; for example, some kingdoms used a 'regnal year' dating from a king's ascension to the throne. The most important calendar at this time in Christian Europe was that of the Church. Saints' days were fixed, but other Church festivals were movable and depended on the date of Easter, which had itself to be calculated with the use of complex tables based on the lunar year and on a factor known as the Golden Number.

The rhythms of the seasons and of the pattern of Christian festivals determined the course of life for the medieval peasant – only governments and scholars concerned themselves with more detailed dating matters. Each season, with its different qualities, was of great importance in the writings of many medieval authors.

Book of Kells (detail), 8th cent. Opening page of St Mark's Gospel.
The decoration of this exquisite manuscript is extremely lavish and imaginative. In 1185, Giraldus Cambensis called it, 'the work of an angel'.

Sixth to ninth centuries

Small Christian communities, independent of Rome, clung to the very margins of the known world at the monasteries founded in Ireland by St Patrick in the mid fifth century. In 563 St Columba and twelve companions set sail for Iona, north-west of Scotland, where he founded the famous island monastery. St Augustine arrived in Britain from Rome in 597, sent by Pope Gregory the Great to bring Christianity to the Anglo-Saxons. The monks who came carried a silver cross and a likeness of Jesus Christ painted on a panel, and these images must have been extremely important to them as they preached to a people who could not understand Latin, nor read in any language. They also brought many books, for Christianity appeared to offer literacy and civilization, and books were essential props, tangible proof of their message. In fact, to the early monks books were quite as important as any of their relics or vestments. The books they brought with them were soon being copied at the new monasteries which they founded up and down the country.

Major works and artists

A very early Psalm book, the Cathach of St Columba, was written in about AD 600 (and is now in the Royal Irish Academy). 'Cathach' means 'fighter', and so it is not surprising to learn that the book was carried into battle as a magic talisman. It is written in Irish half-uncials (uncials are capital letters, and the word 'uncial' comes from the Latin *uncia*, 'inch' – St Jerome referred to 'letters an inch high' as 'uncial') and decorated in a pure Celtic style. It does not contain pictures as such, or decorated borders, but instead has richly ornamented initial letters at the beginning of paragraphs. The simplest of these decorations is the outlining of the letters with red dots, a feature which makes the letters appear to be haloed in a rosy glow. Another characteristic feature is called 'diminuendo'; the large capital letter is followed by a smaller one, and then a smaller one, and so on until a letter the same size as the text is reached.

Abbot Ceolfrith commissioned three Bibles during his time as Bishop at Wearmouth Monastery, Northumbria – one stayed at Wearmouth, one went to Jarrow, and one was intended for presentation to the Pope. This last, now in the Laurentian Library in Florence, is the oldest known complete Latin Bible. The other great English Gospel Books of this time – the *Book of Durrow* (made in about 650), the *Lindisfarne Gospel Book* (made in 698), the *Book of Echternach*, the *Lichfield Gospel Book* and the *Hereford Cathedral Gospel Book*, both made in the West of England in the eighth century – these so-called 'insular' manuscripts are spectacular in their rich ornamentation. Initial letters were filled with designs which were often based on those found on ancient Irish stone crosses and which signified the interconnection of everything. Rich swirls and complicated knotwork fill the voids of the letters and the serifs and terminals are exuberant with animal motifs, braids, chevrons, diamond spirals, and birds. The *Book of Durrow* is not a large book – it is only nine by six inches – but it is filled with wonderfully luxuriant embellishments, coloured with lemon yellow, warm red, and a deep copper green. It contains especially fine carpet pages, whole page abstract, multi-coloured designs of amazing complexity at which the Irish excelled. The historian, Cambrensis, described these illuminations as 'so delicate and subtle ... so full of knots and links with colours so fresh and vivid ... as to be the work of Angels ....'

After the Synod of Whitby in 664, at which the Irish and British declared joint allegiance to the Roman Church, and settled their

Book of Kells, 8th cent. (Dublin, Trinity College): Opening page of St Mark's Gospel.
Tradition has it that the *Book of Kells* was written at St Columba's monastery on the island of Iona.

Book of Kells (detail), 8th cent. (Dublin, Trinity College): Opening page of St Mark's Gospel.
It was said that an angel furnished the designs for this book on a wax tablet, from which the illuminators worked.

differences over their contradictory methods of calculating Easter, the styles of the two areas became more closely associated.

In about 635, the monks of Iona sent St Aidan and his colleagues to found the monastery at Lindisfarne on Holy Island, an inhospitable island off the Northumbrian coast. There the *Lindisfarne Gospel Book* was made, a book which took about two years to complete and is the work of a single scribe, who also did the illuminations. It is a work of outstanding beauty and sophistication, and was possibly meant as a showpiece to display with the body of St Cuthbert, the saintly hermit whose life is so well documented by the Venerable Bede, and who around this time was reburied at Lindisfarne in an elaborate shrine. The book contains a colophon on its last leaf. A colophon was the text which the scribe used to finish the work, much as we might use 'The End' today. Sometimes it included the scribe's name, the date, and the name of the person for whom the book was made. The Lindisfarne colophon was written in about 970, and mentions four participants in the physical making of the book.

As this was written so long after the book was made, it is possible that its contents had long been the stuff of legends. Aldred's Anglo-Saxon gloss is the earliest surviving translation of the Gospels into English. The *Lindisfarne Gospel Book* is the most complete Gospel Book to have survived from the seventh century. It is written in the script known as insular majuscule, and contains marvellous miniatures of the Evangelists, each with his own symbol – the winged man for Matthew, the lion for Mark, the ox for Luke, and the eagle for John. The major decorated pages are composed of pure ornament, amazingly intricate with many varieties of plaits and knotwork, keys, fretwork, and spiral patterns, contorted and interlaced birds and animals. The minor initials are highlighted with dabs of colour, often green or yellow, and outlined with the pink dots which are characteristic of the insular style.

At one time, the *Durham Gospel Book* also belonged to the community of St Cuthbert in Northumbria. There is some evidence that the same hand may have worked on both the liturgical additions to the Lindisfarne Gospels and the corrections to the Durham Gospels: this may mean that a single scriptorium produced both books, or that scholars and scribes moved from place to place; or that the books themselves were sent to different places for critical appraisal. The Echternach Gospels may also have been made at Lindisfarne as a gift for the new foundation at Echternach in Luxembourg in 698. If this is so, the book would have been taken to the Abbey in Luxembourg by St Willibrord and his fellow missionaries. Echternach Abbey then went on itself to fulfil outside orders for manuscripts from communities which lacked the essential skills, or which were perhaps only newly founded, and by the early eleventh century was a leading scriptorium, making manuscripts for the emperors themselves.

The Book of Kells is the most famous, and the latest, of the great Insular Gospel Books. It is written in Irish half uncial, but we do not know for sure whether it was written in Ireland – it may be English or even Scottish, but legend has it that St Columba himself created it in the sixth century on the island of Iona off the West coast of Scotland. The book was in the Abbey of Kells in Ireland, whence the monks of Iona had fled to escape the Vikings, and there the book also survived seven Viking raids between about AD 800 and their final attack in 1006, when the Abbey was burned to the ground. Since 1661 the Gospel Book has been at Trinity College in Dublin, where it may be seen and admired. The book is technically very complex and its manufacture must have been a huge undertaking. Not only does it abound with interpretative pictures with many layers of meaning, all of which help with the visualization of the text, but intellectually the illustrations express insights which Columba was said to have achieved – for example, his association with the Holy Spirit is stressed by decorative emphasis on Christ as being full of Holy Spirit. It is continually decorated throughout with three types of letters: one is decorated with Celtic spirals, triskeles, triquetras; one is filled with highly stylized animal forms (lions are a continuing motif and each letter is unique); and last there is an angular alphabet, very different from the swirling, interlaced letters. The letters are much plainer but contain strong knots, and are sometimes outlined for extra effect. These angular letters also exist in the *Lindisfarne Gospel Book* which, completed in about 698, is much better documented.

In the earliest of days, monasteries were sanctuaries of asceticism, but with the arrival of St Augustine and the complete conversion of the British Isles to Christianity, they gradually became more like training grounds for evangelists ready to spread the word of God. Christianity is very much the religion of the written revelation, and books which had been made for the glory of God alone now took on a slightly different purpose. They were now required as tools for missionaries. And as evangelical Christianity extended back into Europe in the seventh and eighth centuries, so again the purpose of books underwent another change. No longer only the instruments of missionary Christianity, they became also outward symbols of the wealth and power of noblemen and kings.

Ninth to eleventh centuries

Missionaries from the British Isles, having converted the Anglo-Saxons and securely established the rule of Christianity in Britain, carried the word of God back to Europe from about the eighth century, and the books they took with them influenced European artists. Charlemagne,

King of the Franks from 768 and crowned Holy Roman Emperor in 800, saw himself as an emperor in the classical mould, and the beautiful books he collected and caused to be made were part of the trappings of imperial living. These books were indeed exquisite, often written in gold or silver ink on purple-dyed leaves to emphasize his links with imperial antiquity. The Roman satirist Juvenal had said that the Romans dyed parchment red or yellow because white became dirty too easily, and that purple was an extravagance, especially when written with gold or silver. The so-called *Harley Golden Gospels* are written entirely in gold, and although they were probably made near Aachen, Charlemagne's capital city, they show strong traces of English influence alongside the classical. Other books are also highly illuminated with gold, and must thus have been extremely costly. These rare books, several of which were presented by Charlemagne to the abbeys in his empire, were also objects of great monetary value and as such were highly prized diplomatic gifts and visible tokens of the power and splendour of the imperial court. There Germanic warlord tradition met and mingled with the Roman civilization that Charlemagne was nourishing; he had to meet the expectations of his tribal subjects, and valuable books could be seen as loot.

It seems likely that Charlemagne had a genuine interest in learning, though it is debatable whether he himself ever learned to read. He brought to his court many of the known world's greatest scholars, among them the Northumbrian scholar Alcuin, who was then in charge of the cathedral schools in York. Alcuin entered Charlemagne's service as tutor to the royal family, and went on to help inspire the revival of culture at Charlemagne's court. It was Alcuin who, as Abbot of St Martin's Abbey at Tours, established there an especially good Latin text of the Bible, and by the ninth century had begun at Tours the production of illuminated Bibles which was to make the town famous.

One of the reforms Charlemagne undertook during his reign was that of education, and as part of this campaign he introduced a new, simpler, script. This is known as 'Caroline minuscule', and nearly all the manuscripts written during Charlemagne's reign are in this script. The earliest surviving manuscript to contain this script is the Godescalc Evangelistary, commissioned by Charlemagne and completed in 783, which commemorates both the baptism of his son Pepin by Pope Hadrian, and also his fourteenth anniversary as king of the Franks.

When Charlemagne died in 814 his library, so lovingly collected, was sold. Beautiful books continued to be commissioned by Charlemagne's sons and grandsons – his son Drogo owned a Gospel Book written completely in gold, the so-called *Codex Aureus* (the Golden Book) made in 870, whose binding is encrusted with gold and precious stones. These dazzling articles were certainly not for every-

Utrecht Psalter, c. 816 (Utrecht, Bibliotheek der Rijksuniversiteit). Written and illustrated at the great royal monastery of Rheims, the Psalter is written in capital letters and is decorated throughout with little monochrome sketches. The pictures are full of movement, and they give the pages an air of informality and vigour.

CXLVIII ALLELUIA
CANTATE DÑO
CANTICUM NOUUM LAUS
EIUS INECCLESIAS CORUM
LAETETUR ISRAHEL INEO QUI
FECIT EUM ET FILII SION EX
SULTENT INREGE SUO:
LAUDENT NOMEN EIUS IN
CHORO · INTYMPANO
ET PSALTERIO PSALLANT EI ·
QUIA BENEPLACITUM EST

ALLELUIA
DÑO IN POPULO SUO ET EX
ALTABIT MANSUETOS IN
SALUTE ·
EXSULTABUNT SCI IN GLORI
A · LAETABUNTUR INCUBI
LIBUS SUIS ·
EXSULTATIONES DÑI IN GUT
TURE EORUM · ET GLADII
ANCIPITES IN MANIB: EOR
ADFACIENDAM UINDICTA

IN NATIONIBUS · INCRE
PATIONES IN POPULIS ·
AD ALLIGANDOS REGES EORU
INCOMPEDIBUS · ET NO
BILES EORUM IN MANICIS
FERREIS:
UT FACIANT INEIS IUDICIU
CONSCRIPTUM · GLORIA
HAEC EST OMNIBUS SCIS
EIUS ·

day use, but were meant as conspicuous evidence of wealth and power.

After Charlemagne's death and the division of his kingdom among his heirs, it was over 100 years before Otto the Great reunited the empire and again drew attention to learning and religious reform. A shrewd political leader, Otto integrated the state and Church into one administration, and laid great emphasis on the importance of books. However, it was Otto's grandson, Otto III, who, as ruler of Europe at the early age of eighteen, showed real enthusiasm for illuminated manuscripts. He employed no painters at court, but commissioned manuscripts from the great monasteries such as Trier. By then it had become common for laymen to work on these books, although within a monastic environment. One of the artists working in the service of Egbert, Archbishop of Trier (977–993), was the so-called Master of the Registrum Gregorii, whose influence can be found in many contemporary works. At the time of the death in 1024 of Emperor Henry II, Otto's heir, the imperial library contained, among many other volumes, a fifth-century Livy, a copy of Boethius on Arithmetic, the great *Bamberg Apocalypse*, a Gospel Book rich with golden decoration (now in Uppsala University Library) and an illustrated commentary of Isaiah. Various distinctive schools can be distinguished, from the expressionism of Rheims to the more lifelike drawing of the human figure at Aachen.

Major works and artists

It was at Rheims, one of the great royal monasteries, that the famous *Utrecht Psalter* (now in Utrecht University Library) was made. In this Psalter the artists illustrated the Psalms almost line by line, using monochrome line drawings. A copy of the *Utrecht Psalter* found its way to Canterbury, where it was copied several times over the next 200 years. The earliest of these copies is called the *Harley Psalter* and dates from around 1000. In it the flowing line drawings have become multicoloured, a characteristic which was to become typical of Anglo-Saxon manuscripts.

English book painting in the tenth century reached new heights, with Winchester and Canterbury being important centres of manuscript production. One of the masterpieces of this time is the Benedictional made for St Aethelwold, Bishop of Winchester for twenty years from 963. The Benedictional, which we know to have been made by a monk named Godeman, contains the text of the blessings which the Bishop himself would have used at Mass on feast-days. The most important of these feast-days are marked by miniatures containing meticulously drawn figures and foliage extravagantly embellished with gold. Anglo-Saxon England had a remarkably rich literary tradition, in particular in the vernacular; indeed it was the

Benedictional of St Aethelwold, Anglo-Saxon, *c.* 975–980 (British Library): The Nativity.
This benedictional was made for St Aethelwold, for twenty years Bishop of Winchester. The book was made by a monk named Godeman, and contains the text of the blessings which the Bishop himself would have used at Mass on feast-days as well as miniatures richly embellished with gold.

Manuscript of Bury St Edmunds, *c.* 1130 (New York, Pierpont Morgan Library): Church looters.
The monks of Bury St Edmunds were prolific producers of manuscripts in the twelfth century and were noted for the clarity and vigour of their paintings. This miniature conveys a quite extraordinary sense of the tumult accompanying the pillage of the church by the Vikings.

richest in Europe, and included many translations of Latin works as well as original poetry. Aelfric, a pupil of St Aethelwold and later his biographer, translated the first five books of the Old Testament (the Pentateuch), and the versions made at the beginning of the eleventh century are exceptionally rich and varied in their illustrations.

Twelfth century

At this time, the very splendid English monasteries would all have had quite large libraries. We do not know which books they all had, though some of the great foundations kept detailed records which have survived. Of course every monastery would have had at least one Bible, probably more – and sometimes bound in up to four huge volumes. At least one Bible would have been kept in a place accessible by all the monks; they were far too big to be carried around for private use, and in any case a manuscript book was too precious to be carried about. In addition a monastery library might have contained separate books from the Bible each containing a commentary (or 'gloss'); works by churchmen such as St Augustine, Bede, and St Jerome on such subjects as the Psalms; perhaps classical texts such as Livy or Virgil. These works would have helped to build up libraries which were regarded at the time as storehouses, complete with all the information about the world it was possible to have. There would also have been service books of all kinds, from psalters to books of music. The latter, smaller in format, would have been used on a day-to-day basis and copies have not survived in the same way as the great Bibles have. Books which did not fall to pieces in daily use were largely destroyed at the time of Henry VIII's dissolution of the monasteries in 1532, when the liturgy underwent extensive change.

Winchester Bible, 12th cent. (Winchester Cathedral): Initial letter 'O' showing Solomon and the Queen of Sheba. Winchester was an important centre of manuscript manufacture. This Bible uses the Carolingian script introduced by Charlemagne. The colours are bright and clear and the initial is outlined in thick gold bands enclosing blue roundels.

For private worship Psalters were popular, and several survive: one, for instance, from a Psalter probably made at the great nunnery at Shaftesbury, Dorset, for a lady who may have been a nun or who may have been a lay friend of the Abbey; another, a Psalter made for Queen Melisende of Jerusalem in about 1150. Melisende was regent of the kingdom in the Holy Land which had been established as a result of the First Crusade in 1096, and it is clear from the number of manuscripts which survive from this period that Jerusalem must have contained a substantial book-buying population. There were also several religious foundations in and around the city – at least until the kingdom fell to the great Saladin in 1187.

Literacy was still not widespread by the end of the twelfth century, and very little was written that did not have some sort of religious context. The importance of the great religious foundations cannot be over-emphasized – the Benedictines, the Cluniacs, the Cistercians, the Carthusians headed a highly spiritual population. St Benedict (*c.* 480–*c.* 547), who is the founding father of Western monastic life, and of the monastery at Monte Cassino in Italy, had directed members of his Order to read, to make books, and to study. (The oldest surviving copy of his rules for monks is dated AD 700 and is in the Bodleian Library, Oxford.) By 1200 there were over 500 monasteries in England, all in need of books. There must have been a thriving business in book production.

CHAPTER 2

Late Middle Ages

The years of the late Middle Ages were a time of great change and exciting innovation. Merchants were bringing exotic spices and silks from the Orient, architects were designing in challenging new styles, and artists were using new approaches to drawing and painting, including new theories on perspective.

Overleaf:
Christine de Pisan offers her book to
Ysabeau of Bavaria, late 14th cent.
(British Library).
Christine de Pisan wrote delicate love
poetry at a time when France was
witness to a flowering of literature and
the visual arts. The colours in this
miniature are quite gorgeous: the ladies
wearing robes of deep and vibrant hues,
a rich golden ceiling over them, and
little white dogs beside them.

In the thirteenth century the exciting changes that heralded the advent of a new epoch in art, design and culture were echoed in the manuscripts decorated by hand at this time. However, the most exciting change taking place was the broadening scope of education, and the burgeoning of the universities in Europe. For the first time, education was no longer the sole preserve of the Church. The first universities were just informal schools, with a group of students gathered round a teacher. Gradually, however, as the schools expanded they began to take on lives of their own, and as they grew so a massive upheaval took place in the demand and availability of books, in particular textbooks for students. There was still no formal book trade as we might know it and probably books would have changed hands among students themselves unless they were wealthy enough to commission new ones. Paris, as the university there began to come into its own, attracted the craftsmen to satisfy the demand for books. Universities were beginning to find their feet in other European cities too: at Bologna, Oxford and Cambridge, Padua, and Prague.

The Bible was of course the book most sought after. Complete Bibles from this period are rare; it was more often the case that a student would study only one book of the Bible at a time. But as demand grew, Parisian scribes began to put the Bible into a single volume. Obviously for such a large text to fit into one volume the physical book had to be a great deal smaller than the lectern Bibles of the great monasteries, some of which were almost two feet tall.

The names of the books of Bible and their order within the finished text was also standardized at this time, and in addition the books were divided into the chapters we know today (probably by Stephen Langton, who is perhaps better known to us for his drafting of Magna Carta in 1215, and who was working in the cathedral schools of Paris at the turn of the century).

It is clear that by about the middle of the century the book trade was largely in the hands of an organized band of professional, secular manufacturers. In Paris, some booksellers came to be known as university stationers. These stationers owned exemplars of the university textbooks which were unbound and numbered in sequence, with each separate gathering being called a piece, or 'pecia'. It must have been hard work for the scribes to try to keep up with demand, and after about 1250 the 'pecia' system became the norm. Students or professional scribes would borrow only one of these 'peciae' at a time, returning it when he had finished and borrowing the next one in the sequence. This system also allowed a much closer control on the quality of texts by the universities, who operated a system of examinations for accuracy. Contemporary records show that artisans and craftsmen involved in the book trade and manufacture tended to live in adjacent streets in one area of a university city, which must greatly have facili-

fungus de nare fic met dimur;

Early 13th cent. (Oxford, Bodleian Library): Doctor operating on a patient's nose.
This lively picture shows a doctor performing minor surgery on a man's nose. The patient himself has to hold the cup to catch his blood! The picture probably comes from a Herbal or perhaps a medical handbook.

tated the making of books. They produced manuscripts for the schools in the four main areas of scholarship: arts, theology, law and medicine.

Ordinary parish churches too had a great demand for service books of all kinds, as well as for music sheets and other liturgical manuscripts. Because of the great wear to which such books were subjected they were nearly all written on vellum, although at this time paper was becomingly more widely used. Thus as the service books came to be discarded the leaves of vellum were often recycled for other domestic uses such as lining walls; and in this way many have survived today.

A Missal is the service book containing the most solemn service of the Church, Mass, which was celebrated at the altar only by an ordained priest. The illustrations in Missals are not strictly speaking descriptive of the text; the use was perhaps closer to the response of the early monks who considered the image as holy as the text. In the same way, the Sacrament of Bread and Wine *was* the Body and Blood of Christ. As devotional images they represent the Glory of God and were literally to be venerated and worshipped. A wealthy patron for whom a Missal might have been made sometimes had his own coat of arms inserted in the picture, or even a portrait of himself. Often a patron would be a Bishop or other high prelate, but he could also have been a

Arras, Flanders, *c.* 1275–1300
(New York, Pierpont Morgan Library):
The Creation.
This miniature is comprised of four
panels, two of them with a gold
background stamped with panelling
and two with midnight blue. The panels
tell the story of the Creation from
Genesis. The colours are quite
amazingly intense.

Opposite:
Psalter, Flanders, *c.* 1275 (New York,
Pierpont Morgan Library): St Dominic
burning heretics' books.
This miniature comes from a Psalter
made in Bruges around 1275, at a time
when most parish priests would have
owned one. The illustration shows St
Dominic burning the books of the
Albigenses, a heretical sect.

wealthy benefactor of a local church. On the other hand, if a parish had
no patron, the parish priest himself might have had to write and illustrate his own Missal.

The Breviary was the service book for all the other daily services,
Matins, Lauds, Primes and so on, which were to be found in Books of
Hours. Breviaries were used by monks as well as by priests, while only
an ordained priest could use a Missal. Thus Breviaries are either 'secular', which here means, used in a church, or 'monastic', used in a
monastery. There were differences in the text between the two kinds;
and indeed between the Breviaries for the use of different monastic
orders, for example the Benedictines and the Cistercians. It is often
possible to place a Breviary exactly by reference to its mention of feast
days – if a saint particular to an area is given pride of place, then it is
likely that the Breviary was made for that area.

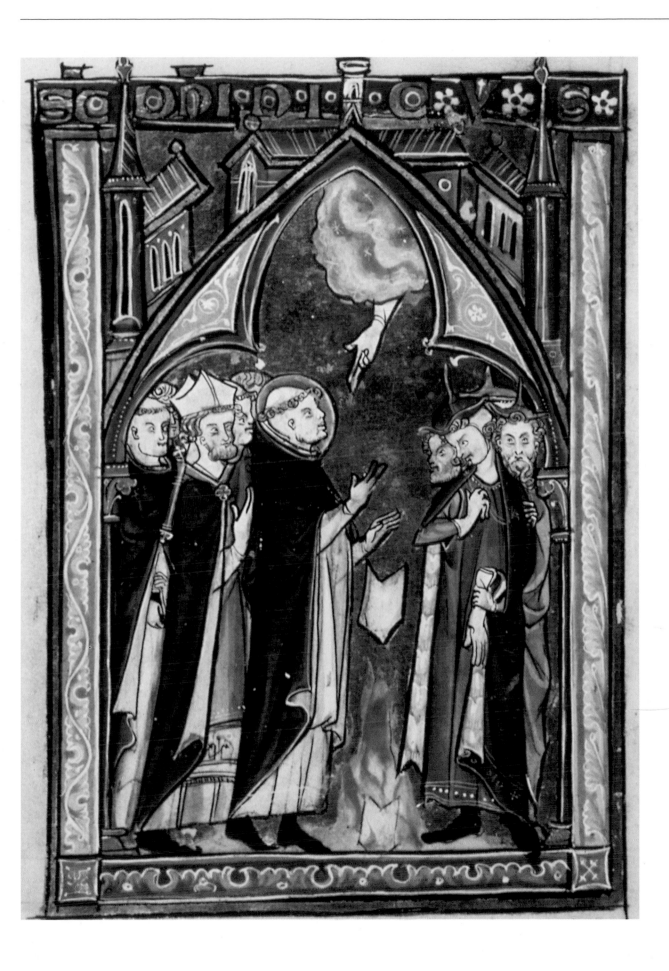

Possibly St Albans, early 13th cent. (Oxford, Bodleian Library): Scribe at his lectern.
St Albans was an important centre for manuscript illumination. Matthew Paris, a monk at the monastery in the first half of the thirteenth century, was one of the most famous artists in Europe.

Opposite:
Psalter of Yolande de Soissons, Amiens, *c.* 1290 (New York, Pierpont Morgan Library): St Francis preaching to the birds.
This portrait shows one of the most famous of the stories associated with St Francis, in which he preaches to birds and animals.

The Bible passage for each day was fixed in the order of service, and it had become convenient for a priest to read the passage from the Missal or Breviary, where it would have been written out in this smaller book for convenience, rather than from a big lectern Bible. These Bibles, usually in Latin but in the Netherlands often in the vernacular Dutch, often comprised more than one volume, and many survive. Thomas à Kempis (1380–1471) author of *The Imitation of Christ*, wrote out a Bible in five volumes, which is now in Darmstadt.

Other service books which were required were Graduals (which are books of music for Mass, and so accompany the Missal), and Antiphoners (which contain the music accompanying the Breviary). Pope Gregory is said to have initiated the music for the liturgy, and many of these music books are beautifully illustrated with brilliant, busy miniatures and borders. They were usually quite large, as they were intended to be displayed on a lectern for use by a choir singing from a single volume. These huge books, with their complicated contents, were still being made by hand in Spain and Portugal long after printing had taken over.

Psalters were also required. Artists round Würzburg in Germany used a very distinctive style with an almost Byzantine appearance and with an unusual use of brown pigment. The lovely *Evesham Psalter* was made for the Abbot of Evesham sometime after 1246. Another Psalter was made by Matthew Paris at the Abbey of St Albans, just outside London and for many years an important centre of manuscript production.

Beautiful Psalters were not only made for the wealthy nobility. Where there was a strong middle class, particularly in England, books were commissioned by well-to-do landowners with no claims to fame (for example, the *St Omer Psalter* made in about 1330 for the St Omer family living at Mulbarton in Norfolk). Another well-known Psalter is the *Luttrell Psalter*, made in Lincolnshire in about 1335 for Sir Geoffrey Luttrell, which is filled with marvellous, vital marginal scenes of everyday life, crop cultivation, cooks at work in the kitchen; vignettes both religious and secular.

A priest not only took services of all kinds in Church, but also undertook many pastoral duties in his parish. He would hear confession, teach what we would call Sunday School, visit the sick and comfort the dying and bereaved. To help him with these duties, he would have possessed small, unassuming books, not illustrated like service books, but very commonly found.

The French royal family was particularly keen on another type of Bible, the Bible moralisée, which was illustrated with pictures of incidents from the Old and New Testaments together with analogous pictures showing the allegorical interpretations. These Bibles contained a great many illustrations and must have been extremely expensive.

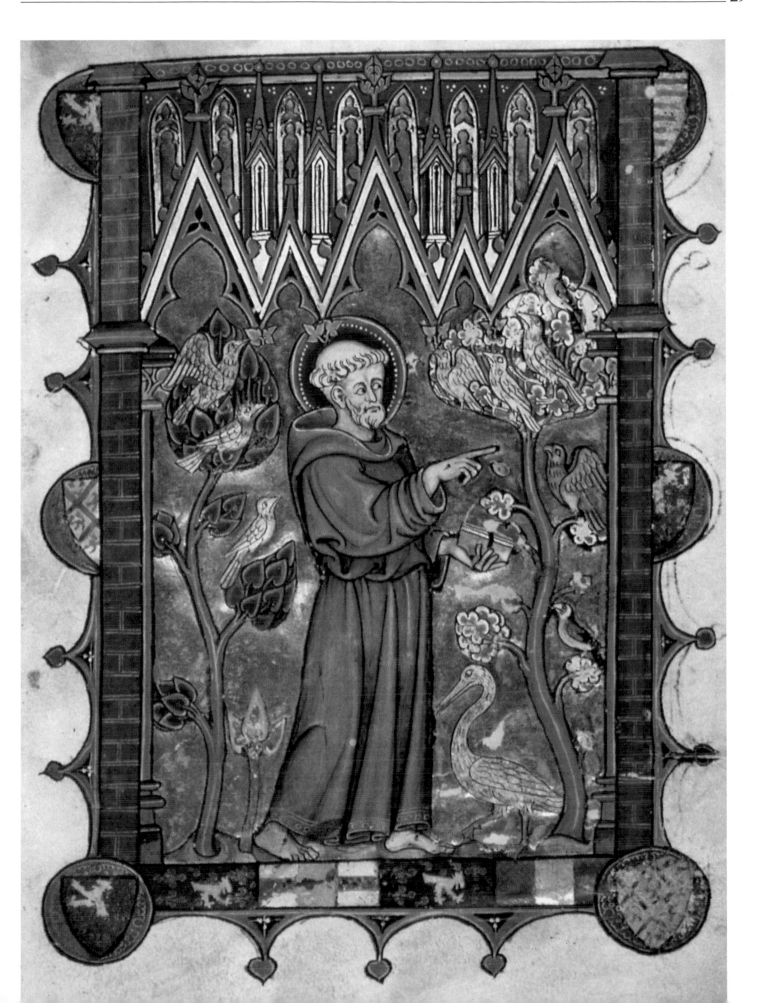

French manuscript, 13th cent. (New York, Pierpont Morgan Library): The Magi before Herod.
The Magi stand before King Herod, who reclines on his throne wearing a richly patterned cloak and brilliant red hose. The borders of the miniature are filled with curling foliage and the colours are muted as befits depiction of such a solemn occasion.

Major works and artists

The Romance of the Rose is the best known French romance of the thirteenth century, a very long allegorical poem describing the adventures of the Lover on his way to winning the love of the Rose. It was written by two poets: the first part of the poem was written by Guillaume de Lorris about 1230, but he abandoned his work, and it fell to Jean de Meun to complete the text, which he did in about 1270.

The poem remained extremely popular over the following centuries, and a great many copies of it have survived, including two which belonged to the Duc de Berry, that very ardent collector of books. Manuscripts of the poem were often beautifully illustrated.

Master Honoré came from Amiens. He worked in Paris between 1288 and 1318, becoming one of the most highly regarded Parisian artists of his day, even being employed by the King. He was influenced by the English style, and worked as a team with his son-in-law Richard of Verdun. He painted an outstanding copy of *La Somme Le Roy*, a treatise on vice composed by the Dominican friar, Père Laurent in 1279, the Breviary of Philip the Fair, and the Legend of St Denis.

William de Brailes lived in Catte Street, Oxford, the street of the illuminators, in the mid thirteenth century. He frequently signed his work, which includes a Book of Hours, one of the earliest in England. He undertook all his own painting, and the decoration is remarkable for the intensity of both design and colouring.

Matthew Paris, a monk at the Abbey of St Albans for over forty years, became famous throughout Europe for the quality of his work. As well as a painter and designer of books, he was also a master sculptor and goldsmith. His unmistakable work can be found in many surviving manuscripts such as his *Historia Major*, now at Corpus Christi College, Cambridge. In his *Chronica Major*, completed in 1258, is a study of an elephant drawn from life; he must have seen the elephant which Louis IX of France presented to Henry III on his return from the Crusades. The beast survived for four years in the special quarters built for it at the Tower of London. Matthew Paris died in 1259.

Historia Major, Matthew Paris, 13th cent. (Cambridge, Corpus Christi College): Battle between Saracens and Christians in Damietta, 1218.
This bloodthirsty battle took place in Egypt during the Fifth Crusade, 100 miles east of Alexandra on the Nile Delta. The prancing horses and dismembered limbs have the extraordinary immediacy of Matthew Paris's new style of line drawing.

Fourteenth century

Since time began, songs have been sung and stories told, round the hearth, to pass the time on journeys, and by professional wandering minstrels. Now, for the first time, these were written down, though in the earliest days the manuscripts were not usually decorated. The gradual increase in the number of people who considered themselves at least slightly literate, and the rise of a wealthy merchant class taking over the powers of the old feudal aristocracy, meant an increase in different kinds of books being produced, and these new types of books were produced with exquisite illustrations. Secular writing flourished throughout Europe, nearly all of it in French, then the language of all educated and sophisticated Europeans, alongside a strong tradition of patronage of manuscript illustrators.

Heroic tales of all kinds were committed to paper, among them the tales of King Arthur and his Knights of the Round Table, the story of *Troilus and Cressida*, accounts of the exploits of Alexander the Great and Charlemagne, the *Song of Roland*, and the German epic poem *Nibelungenlied*. Walter of Henley's *Book of Husbandry* contains descriptions of agricultural tasks, some very detailed. In one, instructions are given for efficient ways of sowing seed, followed by a practical injunction to cover the seed immediately to protect against 'crows, doves and other birds' which would otherwise eat it.

Not only was there a voracious appetite for story books – the fourteenth-century readers also wanted history books, both for instruction and entertainment. They liked tales of Troy, Livy's *Histories*, and almost above all, the *Grandes Chroniques de France,* a highly patriotic text, deluxe copies of which were often given as diplomatic gifts to emphasize the glory of France. As one might expect, the Duc de Berry owned several copies. Other chroniclers include Jean Froissart, who was one of the greatest diarists of the century and the Venetian Marco Polo, who wrote his account of his Travels along the Silk Road in French.

Secular books included Bestiaries, Herbals and Science handbooks, whose illustrations are really crucial to the text – charts of the humours of the body in a science handbook, pictures of plants and animals from Herbals and Bestiaries. The guiding concept of the age was allegory: everything in nature was seen to conceal an allegorical meaning relating to some aspect of Christian doctrine.

Herbals were probably intended for medical and scientific use, and sometimes included a section with a bestiary. The text was an amalgam of botanical and medical bits and pieces and usually gives the characteristics of each plant followed by its medicinal use. While these books were most widely used in the fourteenth century, early examples date from Roman times.

Codex Membrans Chronicles of France,
1388 (British Library): Battle of Crécy.
Many copies of these patriotic
Chronicles were commissioned by the
French royal family for themselves and
as gifts. They contained hundreds of
richly painted miniatures, many
painted by the Boucicaut Master
himself.

Around AD 400 Apuleius Platonicus, a Roman about whom
almost nothing is known, put together the text of a Latin Herbal, using
Greek material. His Herbal was not much more than a fairly thin collection of medical recipes, but over the centuries to come it was very
widely copied. It is likely that the *Herbal of Apuleius* was translated into
Anglo-Saxon around the year 1000, but the first manuscript in translation which has survived dates from around 1050.

About 1120 a manuscript of Apuleius was written and illuminated at the Abbey of Bury St Edmunds, in East Anglia. This text is of
especial interest not because of the Latin text, but because the paintings
of the flowers and herbs are extremely naturalistic, and it is likely that
they were painted from life by a monk who was a true naturalist.

By around 1200 Herbals had ceased to be books which purported
to be useful, and at this time the plants were being depicted in a highly
stylized manner. Some of the manuscripts are really beautiful to look

Jehan de Grise, *Romance of Alexander*, Flanders, *c.* 1338–44 (Oxford, Bodleian Library): Cook and spit.
This secular text was written in French, the literary language of the day, and was a collection of stories and adventures. This marginal illustration shows a cook basting the joint, and obviously feeling the heat from the fire.

at, illuminated with gold and with letters picked out in bright colours; but it would certainly not be possible to use the book for purposes of identification!

The steady deterioration in the standard of botanical illustration continued until almost the end of the fourteenth century as illustrations were copied from book to book and never drawn from life. The increasingly stylized depiction of plants resulted in books of no practical value. By the end of the fourteenth century there was a pressing need for doctors and Herbalists to be able to identify a plant for which they might be hunting. Again southern Italy was in the van of developments. It was then still under Norman rule and also in close contact with the Arab world and its highly developed scientific knowledge, and the first medical school in Europe was founded at Salerno. Texts produced at this time show the rebirth of naturalistic painting, with detail minutely observed, even if the standard of the work is not always very high. Later pictures, still beautifully coloured and gilded, came to include figures, landscapes, and scenes filled with bustling activity. The emphasis shifted slightly so that the texts were now aimed more at instruction for the living of a healthy life, and many were copies of manuscripts available in Arabic – at the monastery of Monte Cassino the monks translated texts from both Arabic and Greek.

Illustrations of a completely different order fill a Herbal of about 1400, an Italian translation of yet another Arabic work, a treatise on medical botany by Serapion the Younger, who had completed his work 600 years earlier. These exquisite pictures are completely lifelike, graceful and delicately coloured. The text which runs alongside them has letters picked out in red and blue, but not so ornate as to detract from the plants, which irresistibly draw the eye. History does not record the name of the artist.

A curiosity in the field of Herbals is the so-called 'Roger Bacon Cipher Manuscript'. This text is written in a cipher which has confounded every cryptographer and is to this day unsolved. It contains many quite unnaturalistic drawings and paintings of flowers, together with depictions of a pestle and mortar and thus may be taken for a Herbal; but it also contains a great many other drawings of an extremely eccentric character, mainly astrological but also several showing little plump nude women, seemingly having a bath amid complicated plumbing. It is thought at one time to have been in the library of John Dee, the English magician and mathematician; perhaps it is really a treatise on alchemy.

By the beginning of the sixteenth century the illustrations in Herbals began to feature not only medicinal and otherwise useful plants, but also pictures of flowers included for their good looks only. By this time several printed Herbals already existed, but exquisite manuscripts were still being produced for bibliophiles and collectors. With illustrations influenced by the popularity of lavish Books of

Psalter of Queen Mary, early 14th cent. (British Library): Harvesters under a supervisor.
This Psalter, the work of a single English artist, contains an astonishing number of illustrations – tinted drawings of Old Testament subjects, full-coloured miniatures from the New Testament, and characteristic panel scenes such as this one showing the feeding of pigs.

Hours, manuscripts contain delightful paintings replete with insects, snails and small animals, painted in glowing, jewel-like colours.

Bestiaries, compendiums of information about animals, were all originally based on a Latin translation of a Greek compendium called *The Naturalist*. The earliest surviving illustrated text was made in Rheims, Northern France, in about 840, and Bestiaries in many languages remained popular well into the fifteenth century. The animals depicted were of three types: familiar – horses, dogs, cats; exotic – elephants, lions, camels; and imaginary – manticores, dragons, griffins, phoenixes. All these animals were presented with equal conviction, for direct observation and the use of first-hand experience were not typical ways of acquiring information in the Middle Ages; seeing was not required for believing, and it is clear from the descriptions of the beasts that medieval interest in animals was based largely on their usefulness as symbols, particularly for allegorical purposes. Fact was squarely placed in the service of the Church. The characteristics and habits assigned to each animal – both real and imaginary – by the writer of a Bestiary were devised to make them effective as moral examples. In fact, the emphasis the writers placed on symbolism and moral edification make the accuracy of their information, or even the actual existence of the animal, less important than the beast's moral usefulness.

As well as employing his imagination, the medieval artist, usually an anonymous artisan, turned for inspiration to those ever-popular sources, Greek and Roman literature. He was not expected to have an original style; his method of working was to perfect his technique and to reuse whatever would be useful within a Christian context. However, there seems to be no end to the fantastic creatures that artists did invent; basilisks, manticores, bonnacons, serras, and many variations of dragons and serpents. The illuminations in Bestiaries are often brightly coloured, with copious use of red, blue or green – colours not normally associated with animals. The text is usually in two parts. In the first, the animal's name, habitat, and physical characteristics are explained; in the second these attributes are interpreted to provide allegorical meanings. For example, the camel is noted as being able to endure thirst for long periods and to drink large quantities at a time against future need: thus he becomes a symbol of prudence and temperance.

It was not until the thirteenth century that a more scientific approach began to be taken to natural history, in particular by Frederick II, Holy Roman Emperor from 1212, a religious sceptic and often considered the most cultured man of his time. He wrote a treatise called *The Art of Hunting with Birds* around 1250, which is a major work on ornithology complete with systematic data collection and recording. The change in approach to natural history can also be seen in

Hours of Catherine of Cleves, Master of Catherine of Cleves, *c.* 1440 (New York, Pierpont Morgan Library): The Holy Family at work.
Catherine's Book of Hours was made for her in Utrecht in about 1440 by an unknown artist. This is a delightful domestic scene of the Holy Family – Mary weaves, Joseph is at his woodwork, and the infant Jesus is toddling in a baby walker, which surely Joseph must have made for him.

eus in adiutoriũ meũ
antende. dñe ad adiuuã
dum me festina. Glo
na patri. Siat erat. v̄. ym̄
e causa mundiae sue.
neɔnon sanctitatis. car
nem me misere sumpsit
ut humanitatis. peperit regem

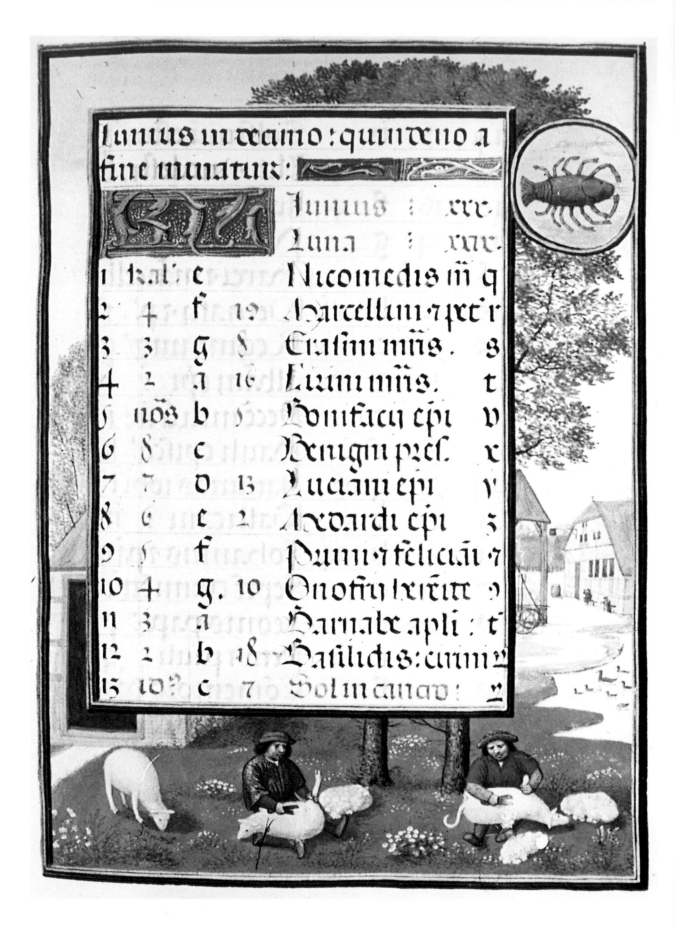

Bartholomeus Anglicus's encyclopaedia of animals, which omits the allegorical information; and in a book by Brunetto Latini, which omits most of the imaginary animals. Later still, Richard de Fournival's *Bestiary of Love* is a secular work of social satire, and as the Church began to lose its monopoly of the world view, direct observation and deductive reasoning began to gain ground.

The fourteenth century also saw Italian literature assured of its place; Dante Alighieri's *Divine Comedy,* written in the Tuscan dialect of Italian in the first quarter of the century, is one of the world's greatest classics. Over a thousand manuscripts exist, including one made for the royal library of Aragon and one illustrated by Botticelli. Boccaccio wrote the first biography of Dante, and also copied out the *Divine Comedy* as a gift for Petrarch. His *Decameron*, written in about 1350, was an instant success and was later extensively mined by both Chaucer and Shakespeare. He owned a fine library which he bequeathed to the Augustinian convent of Santo Spirito in Florence. He was a dedicated patron of literature, and encouraged many young writers and collectors, among them Poggio Bracciolini (1380–1459) and Niccolo Niccoli (*d.* 1437).

The Florentine Francesco Petrarch (1304–74), also a friend of Boccaccio, is widely regarded as the founder of Italian humanism. Not only was he a great writer in his own right (his poems, inspired by the unknown Laura, influenced lyric poetry as far away as Tudor England), but he was also a well-known collector of books.

In around 1400 Poggio, another Italian humanist, with his humanist friends, devised a new style of manuscript. He used a single column, not a double, and took pains to make the script as clear as possible. He took as his example the minuscule of his books dating from the Carolingian period, a script which he called '*lettera antica*' and which he admired not only because it was clear but because it was old. He filled the initial letters with a swirling pattern of white vine stems and leaves which has come to be known as the humanist vine, but which was based on twelfth-century models. The pattern is also reminiscent of the acanthus leaves which appear in Roman decoration (and which, in later centuries, the Victorians also admired and used widely in their architecture). This new style held enormous appeal for scholars and collectors alike.

The atmosphere of commitment to classical learning and scholarship was to nourish the young Cosimo de' Medici (1389–1464) in his passion for erudition and culture in all forms. He must have been especially welcome by his friends the Florentine book collectors, because unlike them he was an extremely wealthy man and he could afford to buy the manuscripts which they could not.

As private collections increased in Italy, more and more people became involved, and gradually what had begun as a personal

Book of Hours, Flemish, *c.* 1525 (Oxford, Bodleian Library): Shearing sheep.
This is the page for June from the calendar at the beginning of the Book of Hours listing saints' days. Special days were written in red – 'red letter days'. Two shepherds each hold a sheep on their knee and cut through the fleece with the heavy shears called forces.

enthusiasm almost imperceptibly changed into a professional book trade. One man who we know to have been involved is Vespasiano da Bisticci (1422–98), a bookseller who acted for Cosimo de' Medici on many occasions, and who also employed scribes and undertook through them the manufacture of books to order. Although Bisticci must have been a large and important employer, some of the scribes were only working part-time – they were notaries, perhaps, or priests, educated men who were supplementing their incomes. Many scribes at this time signed and dated their work, and even added personal notes to the reader.

The greatest English author of this time was of course Geoffrey Chaucer, blazing a trail as a writer in English. *The Canterbury Tales* is his masterpiece, an incomparable piece of social observation, but he also wrote an English translation of *The Romance of the Rose* and a version of the story of *Troilus and Cressida*. About eighty contemporary manuscripts of *The Canterbury Tales* survive; many of them are illuminated but only the well-known *Ellesmere Chaucer* contains any significant illustrations. English secular texts were seldom illustrated, perhaps because aristocratic patronage of the arts scarcely existed in England at that time. England also lagged behind France and Italy in the matter of a professional book trade – a guild of scribes and illuminators was not formed until early in the fifteenth century – and there were no bookshops similar to those in, for example, Paris or Bologna.

The *Brut*, a history chronicle written in French verse for an aristocratic audience and added to by various chroniclers, was available in English by about 1330. The other great history book of the day, the *Polychronicon*, was written, in Latin, by Ranulph Higden, the monk in charge of the library at St Werburg's Monastery in Chester and one of the most knowledgeable chroniclers of his day. The *Polychronicon* also includes geographical information, stories of miracles, and information of all kinds. The Benedictine Order, to which Higden belonged, laid great emphasis on reading and writing – indeed, a meeting of the governing body of the Benedictines in 1277 laid down that the monks should 'study, write, correct, illuminate and bind books according to their capacities rather than labour in the fields'. In 1387 the book was translated into English by John Trevisa. William Caxton took a small part of Higden's *Polychronicon* and reprinted it in 1480 as his *Description of Britain*.

Poems such as *Piers Plowman* and *Sir Gawain and the Green Knight* are allegories with Christian messages, and love poetry often used its themes to discuss the love of Christ; a famous example is the *Song of Solomon*. Other devotional works might contain illustrations depicting religious themes by reference to everyday life, for example, a picture of a lady in a cart on stony road might indicate the soul's rough journey through life.

Book of Hours of Antoine de Navarre,
15th cent. (Oxford, Bodleian Library):
Death at home.
This densely decorated page is the opening of the Office of the Dead and shows the last rites being administered to a dying man. The border is packed with flowers and birds of every hue, and two smaller miniatures within roundels.

an. placebo. ps.
ilexi quoniam
exaudiet domin

Major works and artists

Jean de Bruges worked at the French court for King Charles V between 1368 and 1381. His work helped to make Paris the unrivalled centre for manuscript illumination. Jacquemart de Hesdin was among the most famous of French illuminators working at the end of the fourteenth century. He was in the service of the Duc de Berry for many years, and collaborated on the Duke's superb Books of Hours.

Thomas Rolf is the maker of the famous *Lytlington Missal*, made in about 1384 for Abbot Thomas Lytlington of Westminster Abbey in London. It has particularly beautifully historiated initials (initials with figures and stories drawn inside, see page 56).

John Sifer was a Dominican friar who signed several of the illuminations in the great *Sherborne Missal*, made for the Abbey of Sherborne in Dorset around 1400. He also painted a Lectionary which contains a self-portrait and a portrait of his patron, Lord Lovell.

Fifteenth to sixteenth centuries

This was the heyday for those most famous of medieval books, Books of Hours. Little books, usually lavishly illustrated and produced for the wealthy, were intended to help the devout to pray at home. They were meant to be used and admired, often by people who had never before owned a book, and they were made in huge quantities to meet the demand. Bruges became a noted centre for manuscript illumination, with books made there exported to England, Rome, and Spain.

It can be very difficult to date a Books of Hours, and not many are signed by their makers. A buyer would probably have commissioned a volume through a bookseller. He could choose the texts he wanted included – or those he could afford – from examples held in stock by the bookseller, and the manuscript would then be written and decorated by a team of artists. Part of the skill of the artist would be to execute a known subject with careful devotion to familiar precedents; he was not expected to produce an original composition but to work to a specific formula.

Many at this time of increased piety were keen to perform their devotions privately at home as well as going to Mass. The central figure of the Books of Hours was the Virgin Mary who, then as now, was seen as more powerful than the saints but more approachable than God. The Middle Ages were a time of preoccupation with eternal life, and Books of Hours emphasize this. They contained devotional texts – prayers, hymns, readings, and psalms – meant to be read in private at each of the canonical hours of the day: Matins, Lauds, Prime, Terce, Sext, None, Vespers, and Compline. In addition Books of Hours contained a calendar of the Church year, with saints' days (ordinary

Chronicles, Froissart, 15th cent. (British Library): Messire de Craon received by the Duke of Brittany.
Froissart describes in his vivacious *Chronicles* the exploits of the sophisticated and adventurous French-speaking aristocracy of Europe. This illustration shows Pierre de Craon arriving with his cousin, the Duke of Brittany, possibly having fled after his failed assassination attempt on the life of Olivier de Clisson, Constable of France, in 1392.

saints' days were usually written in black and special ones in red – hence 'red-letter day'), the Office of the Dead, and other readings and prayers. Because each book was unique and included regional variations in illustration and liturgy, it is sometimes possible to find out where a book was originally made by looking for local peculiarities.

Some households went on to use their Hours as a record of family deaths and births. If children were taught to read, the Hours was probably their primer and may well have been the only book they were ever to read; the texts they contained must have been known by heart to half Europe. They were produced in all the main European languages and in their illustrations is a wealth of incidental detail alongside the strictly devotional images.

These illustrations, both beautiful and full of information about the medieval world, frequently depicted the traditional Labours of the Months, the conventional activities of each month of the year as shown in classical art and literature. The original Labours of the Months were a sequence of activities undertaken by mythological figures shown on Roman calendars. The Labours were generally depicted as being much the same whether the Book of Hours was for a nobleman in the north of England or a patron in southern Italy, despite the very different climates and conditions, demonstrating that the classical influence was stronger than that of personal observation. In the Middle Ages the Christian faith, so good at using classical models to make its own point, overlaid the originals.

Typical of the principal activities shown are digging in the fields and cultivating flowers in the spring, harvesting or threshing in the summer, the wine harvest and provisioning against the winter with the slaughter of an ox or pig in the autumn, and for winter a blazing fire to sit beside as snow lies on the ground outside. There are highly detailed paintings of rural activities such as shepherds tending their flocks or acorns being shaken from trees for the fattening of pigs; there are also borders surrounding the text which are filled with exquisite depictions of animals and flowers, delicately painted butterflies, snails, or ladybirds, as well as bustling cameos of village life.

In these Books of Hours, precise observation and refined detail result in paintings of an almost photographic quality. They were huge bestsellers and must have given great aesthetic pleasure to their owners as well as devotional assistance. The patronage of noblemen such as the Duc de Berry must also have helped to make these little books fashionable.

Henry V and his English armies defeated the French at Agincourt in 1415. In 1420, after further successive victories, he entered Paris as regent of France and heir to the French throne. The occupation was to last for seventeen years, and must have been disruptive to daily life. It seems that many book illustrators fled to the provinces: this also

helped to spread the popularity of Books of Hours. For example, the painter known as the Fastolf Master appears to have moved to Rouen, and later (about 1440) went to London, taking his style and models with him. It was a full thirty years before illustrators began to drift gradually back to Paris.

The Duke of Bedford, Henry V's brother and on Henry's death in 1422 his successor as military commander in France, married Anne, sister of the Duke of Burgundy, in order to cement an alliance between England and France. Bedford was a connoisseur of fine books, and among other books in his library he had a magnificent Psalter which had been illuminated in England by Herman Scheerre. The latter was German, but he worked in England for most of his career, where his style was extremely influential.

Sir John Mandeville's Travels was a fictional account composed around the middle of the fourteenth century in the Netherlands. It was probably originally written in French but was soon translated into several other languages. It was likely originally meant as a *vade mecum* for pilgrims to the Holy Land, but it also included legends and stories, and was hugely popular – many more copies of it have survived than of Marco Polo's *Travels*. In one manuscript of the *Travels*, made in Austria, each of the pages is in *grisaille* (monochromatic painting), tinted a delicate green. Only the faces and hands of the characters and the sky are differently coloured.

Manuscript, *c.* 1550 (Rouen Library): Henri II of France enters Rouen. Henri II is remembered for taking Calais back from the English, prompting Mary Tudor to say that when she died the word 'Calais' would be found written on her heart. Henri married Catherine de' Medici, who after his death was responsible for the murder of the Huguenots at the Massacre of St Bartholomew in 1572.

Manuscript, Coetivy Master, *c.* 1455 (New York, Pierpont Morgan Library): Boetius, Philosophy and the Seven Sciences.
The fifth-century Roman philosopher Severinus Boetius is shown in contemporary fifteenth-century idiom. Boetius wrote treatises on music and mathematics as well as a dialogue in prose, *The Consolation of Philosophy*.

Opposite:
Book of Hours of Anne of France, Jean Colombe, 1480–1485 (New York, Pierpont Morgan Library): Adam and Eve.
Behind this scene is an exquisite summer landscape painted by Jean Colombe, the artist who finished the Duc de Berry's *Très Riches Heures* when it was left unfinished in 1416 on the deaths of the Limbourg brothers.

Italy in the fifteenth and sixteenth centuries was a land of independent city states – Venice, Florence, the papal states. The spiritual heirs of Petrarch, the humanist Felice Feliciano (1432-80) of Verona had a fervent passion for ancient Roman culture, and together with the artist Andrea Mantegna and Marco Zoppo would copy out the texts on any Roman inscriptions he could find, and decorate them. They abandoned the white vine and the interlacing borders filled with cherubs, birds, and flowers, and instead filled their illuminations with Roman motifs such as military standards, shields, and coins. The new style soon became extremely popular throughout Italy.

Major works and artists

Perhaps the most famous Book of Hours is the *Très Riches Heures* made for the Duc de Berry (and now in the Museé Condé at Chantilly), but in fact it is untypical of Books of Hours exactly because it is so grand. The three Dutch Limbourg brothers, Pol, Herman, and Hennequin, produced what must be their finest work in this book. Nothing like it had been produced before. In its sensitive attention to every rich detail the calendar gives us a vivid sense of the countryside at different times of the year – the snow lying under a leaden sky for February, boys splashing in a pond in August, summer sun beating down on the

Probably Simon Marmion, *c.* 1480 (New York, Pierpont Morgan Library): Massacre of the Innocents.
This illustration is rich with contemporary detail of clothing and architecture. The border has a golden background scattered with flowers in the style made popular by the atelier of Alexander Bening, working at Ghent and Bruges.

Opposite:
Book of Hours, Bedford Master, *c.* 1420 (New York, Pierpont Morgan Library): Annunciation.
Mary is reading her own book of devotions and is greeted by the angel Gabriel with the news that she is to become the mother of the Saviour. The border is especially densely decorated with flowers and ribbons, and coats of arms of the original owner of the book.

harvest in July, men and women toasting themselves before the fire or tending their sheep in the snowy fields in January. The sacred stories too are intense with the sensation of immediacy. In the painting of Christ in Gethsemane, a gentle night encompasses Christ, and the soldiers faint at the sight of Him.

The painter has used the technique called *grisaille* for this moving night-time image. The starry sky behind is diapered and gilded. The mood is unforgettable, marvellously moving. The Limbourgs obtained especially beautiful effects by adding gold emulsion to the usual colours, or by glazing gold leaf with red or green pigments – water in particular has a sheen and transparency provided by glazing silver leaf with green. Gold is used mainly for the ecclesiastical images, the most precious metal is most closely associated with God. The brothers were also responsible in this marvellous canon of paintings for a new naturalistic style, with the depiction of shadows on the ground or on water and the clever use of differences in colour and tone to show perspective.

The book was unfinished at the deaths in 1416 of the Duc de Berry and all three of the Limbourgs. It was completed by Jean Colombe, an artist who dominated the last days of French manuscript illumination and whose work is a grand finale for the manuscript art of the Middle Ages.

The Duc de Berry owned other Books of Hours, all almost equally celebrated: for instance, the *Belles Heures* and the *Petites Heures*. Another exquisite Book of Hours is the *Hastings Hours*, made in Flanders in about 1480 for William Lord Hastings. It contains border decorations of exquisite delicacy, with flowers and butterflies so lifelike it seems possible to pick them up off their golden background. Hastings sadly had not long to enjoy his book; he was executed in 1483 by the Duke of Gloucester, subsequently King Richard III.

Simon Bening of Bruges (1483–1561) was the most celebrated Flemish manuscript illuminator of the second generation of the famous Bruges/Ghent school. He was the son of Alexander Bening, also a well-known illuminator with a substantial atelier. In old age he painted his self-portrait, standing by a leaded window and holding his spectacles. Characteristic of the style of his atelier are the extremely lifelike flowers and insects scattered on luminous gold borders which can be seen in several Books of Hours, including those for Queen Isabella the Catholic, and the *Hastings Hours*. Simon Bening specialized in Books of Hours, and his landscapes are particularly fine and filled with detail.

The Boucicaut Master takes his soubriquet from a Book of Hours containing over forty miniatures made about 1405 for the Maréchal de Boucicaut, Marshal of France. He was perhaps Jacques Coene, working in Paris between about 1398 and 1404. About thirty Books of Hours are

ascribed to his atelier, including two which are dated by the inclusion of a note that they were made in 1408, the year in which the bridges of Paris were washed away. His style can also be discerned in very many other paintings, including several secular texts such as the *Grandes Chroniques de France* , and he must have headed a busy workshop. A workshop such as this used pattern sheets for the most commonly required illustrations for a Book of Hours. Apprentices could have copied them out very quickly.

The *Bedford Psalter*, made about 1420, contains margins filled with roundels featuring mythical beasts, portraits, and heraldic shields. Bedford also had a celebrated Breviary and a Book of Hours, both

Opposite:
Bedford Hours, 15th cent. (British Library): Legend of the Fleur de Lys. This Book of Hours was made for John, Duke of Bedford, and from 1422 Regent of France, at a leading Parisian atelier. The foremost illustrator is now known as the Bedford Master, a man of exceptional ability with colour and landscape, and illuminator of many codices.

Book of Hours of Cardinal Alessandro Farnese, Giulio Clovio, 1546 (New York, Pierpont Morgan Library): Adam and Eve, the Temptation.
Giulio Clovio was born in Croatia but worked chiefly in Rome, the most celebrated miniaturist of his time. This book, made for Cardinal Farnese, is a lavish codex in an ornate and intricate style.

made by the artist we call the Bedford Master. The Bedford Master was perhaps Jean Haincelin, working in Paris from 1403 to 1448. He too can be seen as one of the artists who worked on the Books of Hours made in 1408, the year the Seine flooded. His workshop also used patterns, modifying illustrations from various sources and using them over and over again. He takes his name from the *Bedford Hours*, produced for John, Duke of Bedford (brother of Henry V, the victor of Agincourt), who married Anne, sister of the Duke of Burgundy.

Bartolomeo Sanvito (1435–c. 1511) was a scribe from Padua. He excelled at the new type of illustration, and used beautiful clear script, trompe-l'oeil borders, and elegant capital letters. He was a great friend of the humanist collector Bernardo Bembo, and was a respected antiquarian and bibliophile. He worked at the Papal Court from 1469 to 1501.

The Master of Catherine of Cleves, who was Dutch, is so called for a Book of Hours painted about 1440 for Catherine Duchess of Cleves. He also worked on other Dutch vernacular Bibles, and is noted for having worked in line drawings as well as paintings.

Jean Bourdichon of Tours was a Court painter, and is noted for his miniature portraits often framed in gold and with a striking air of tranquillity. He was a master of perspective. To him is attributed the *Hours of Anne of Brittany*, one of the most splendid Hours ever made. The borders are filled with elegantly drawn flowers, each identified not only in French but also in Latin. He died in 1521, not long after working on designs for the Field of the Cloth of Gold, Francis I and Henry VIII's famous meeting at Guisnes in 1520.

Giulio Clovio was born in Croatia but worked chiefly in Rome, the most celebrated miniaturist of his time. This book, made for Cardinal Farnese, is a lavish codex in an ornate and intricate style. Vasari, the Italian painter and art historian, described Clovio as 'the Michelangelo of small works'.

DEVS·IN·ADIVTORIV̄
MEVM·INTENDE

DOMINE·AD·ADIVVA
NDVM·ME·FESTINA

CHAPTER 3

Materials and Manufacture

'Illuminated' technically means decorated with metals, gold or silver, which catch the light and literally illuminate the manuscripts. These days the term more generally describes those richly decorated books made by hand during the medieval period.

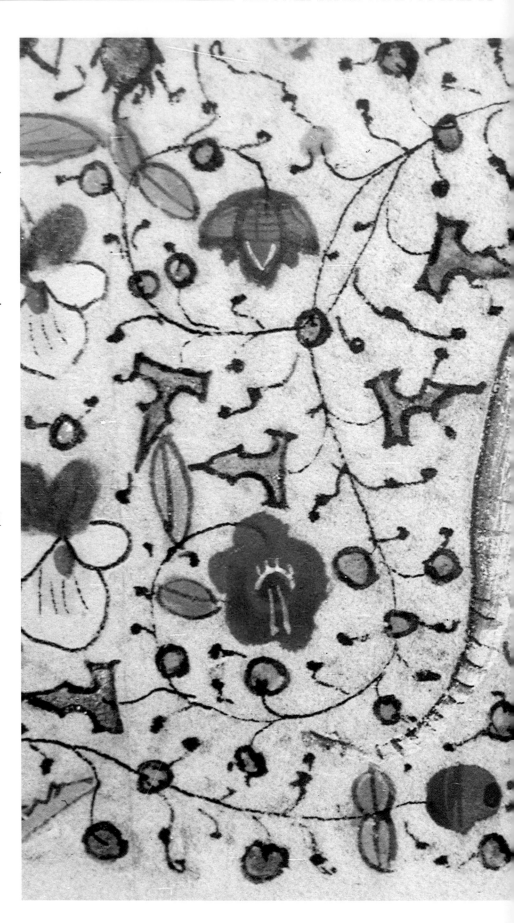

Books are highly durable articles, and many thousands have survived, even many of the very oldest of all. Each is of course different, not only because each was painstakingly made and illustrated by hand but because of the great variety of end uses.

The folded and sewn manuscript book, as distinct from a scroll, is called a 'codex'. The word codex comes from the Latin *caudex* meaning 'tree trunk' or 'bark'. The medieval codex in the West was derived from three discrete ornamental elements – the initial letter, both large and small, the border decoration, and the miniature. Elaborately decorated initial letters were in use from the seventh century, when the British Gospel Books contained a richly calligraphic ornamentation of inter-laced ribbons, foliage, and stylized birds and animals. The arrange-ment of the capital letters gradually extended into the borders of the text until the borders became features in their own right. The figures drawn inside the initial letters developed, too, and gradually became small scenes – stories, hence the term 'historiated initial'.

These little pictures were often of high distinction. The word 'miniature' comes from the Latin word meaning 'to colour in red'; red was one of the earliest colours to be used in codices and gradually the term came to signify all the pictures which accompany the text in manuscript books.

All manuscripts from the fifth to the thirteenth centuries were written on vellum, which is the same thing as parchment. It is made from animal skin, perhaps most usually the skin of a sheep or cow. Goatskin was used too, and probably also deer or pigskin – in fact, whatever animal was commonly to hand. In the seventh and eighth centuries, monasteries would have used parchment from their own animals, collecting skins over a period in order to have enough, though they probably had to buy extra skins if they were undertaking a really big book. Sometimes locally made vellum was not up to scratch and in some books (for example, a Bible made for the monastery of St Alban's in 1135) we can see that illustrations have been made on separate pieces of parchment and dropped in. Professional parchmenters, highly skilled experts at their trade, are documented from at least 822, when Abbot Adelard of Corbie in France is recorded as having a parch-ment-maker on the payroll of the monastery. A good parchmenter, a man in a trade which expanded greatly over the next 500 years, would be able to take a skin and transform it into a soft, supple, white material for writing on. The process, both time-consuming and complicated, scarcely changed over 800 or 900 years.

First, the parchmenter would select good skins, paying close attention to colour and quality. The next step was to soak the skins in a lime solution for several days and then scrape off all the hair. Once the skin was cleaned, it was fixed with pegs on to a frame to dry. Then the parchmenter would take a crescent-shaped knife called a lunellum

Franciscan Calendar, workshop of Jean Colombe, 1481–95 (Lyon, Bibliothèque Municipale): Bringing down acorns. This miniature is at the bottom of a page of saints' days in a Calendar used by the Franciscan order and made in Bourges at the workshop of the celebrated Jean Colombe. Peasants are knocking acorns out of the trees for winter feed for their pigs.

(there are many depictions of these knives in contemporary miniatures) and scrape energetically at both surfaces of the skin. With the round blade of this special knife the parchmenter would run less risk of cutting or tearing the skin, now stretched taut on its frame and of course shrinking as it dried. (If the skin did tear, the cut could be stitched; but there are manuscripts in which the parchment contains a hole, and the scribe has carefully written round it.) The scraping and stretching continued until the parchment was at the right thickness (the little Bibles being made in fourteenth-century Paris used parchment which was almost tissue thin). The dry sheets of vellum were then either rolled or cut to shape and stored for use. The grain side, where the hair used to be, is usually darker in colour and more velvety.

Good parchment was extremely expensive, and on several medieval manuscripts it can be seen that the parchment has been re-used – religious and secular works alike could be erased by soaking the parchment in milk and then scraping to remove the ink and pigment. It is sometimes possible to recover the lost writing by the use of chemicals or ultraviolet light, especially as it was sometimes not thoroughly erased. These re-used leaves are called *palimpsests*.

The size of the animal governed the ultimate size of the sheet of vellum and so the ultimate size of the book being produced. One sheepskin was folded twice to make four pages of an early Gospel book; so a book with 100 pages represented twenty-five animals.

Before parchment came into common use, texts had often been written on papyrus, a cheap reed material used by the Greeks and the Egyptians. This was a good material for scrolls, but not for a bound book, as the material was too fragile to withstand the constant turning of pages or the sewing of the gatherings on to the binding. However, *papyrus* survives in a way, as the word is the ancestor of our word 'paper'.

Paper was invented in China in about the second century, and although there were paper mills in France by about the middle of the fourteenth century, it was not until the end of the fifteenth century that paper manufacture became common in England. By the fifteenth century, plenty of books were being written on paper, though most people thought paper would not last as long as parchment. Actually, although parchment is extremely durable and strong, so is good-quality linen rag paper. The invention of the printing press changed everything; and although luxury handmade books and some legal documents continued to be produced on parchment, cheap books printed on paper became the norm everywhere.

Hymn Book, French, 1586 (Oxford, Bodleian Library).
This is a double-page spread from a Hymn Book in French given to Queen Elizabeth I by Georges de la Motte. It is bordered with coloured roundels and shields containing entwined initials and the arms of the Queen, and there is a regal miniature of the Queen herself.

Paper was made from linen rags in the Middle Ages, with Italy being the main exporter of paper to other European countries. The rags were chopped, then soaked for a few days until they became a pulp; then a thin layer would be scooped up into a wire frame like a sieve and allowed to drip dry. This sheet would be tipped out on to a layer of felt, another layer of felt placed on top, another of paper, another of felt, and so on. The stack would then be weighted and left to dry. Each sheet of paper would then be 'sized' with animal glue, probably made from boiled bones or skin or both, to make it smoother and less absorbent. By the fourteenth century paper-makers in Europe had also discovered that a little pattern twisted into the wire of the frame would transfer to the paper as it dried, and they came to use these 'water-marks' as the distinguishing marks of the paper produced at their own workshops. All kinds of engaging designs were used, from animals and flowers to astrological symbols, from religious emblems to scissors and spectacles.

Very early manuscripts were simply several sheets laid one on top of the other, and folded down the middle. However, unless the book is very small this does not make a convenient article to hold, and very soon books came to be made in the same way as they are today. The book is assembled out of smaller gatherings sewn together. Each gathering, or signature (as it is still called today), was usually made up of eight leaves. This method of binding would also have meant that each signature could have been worked on by a different scribe or artist, which would of course have increased the speed at which the work could be undertaken.

Books were made under very varied conditions – in the earliest days they were probably written by monks sitting outside, with the gatherings of leaves of vellum on their knees, but later, when more books were being produced there was probably a special room in a monastery called a *scriptorium*.

Each page would then have to be prepared for writing by the ruling of guide lines, and the arranging of the page into the number of columns to be used. There was also a precise formula to be followed for working out the relationship between the margins and the text area. Until the twelfth century, rules would have been scored with a dry, pointed implement such as a stylus rather than drawn with ink. By the twelfth century, lines were being drawn using what looks like graphite but is probably metallic lead, and from the thirteenth century lines were ruled in ink, often coloured ink, and sometimes even a combination of colours. In order to keep the grid of lines the same from page to page, the scribe would take a stack of leaves, rule out the top one, and then, using a sharp spike such as an awl would prick right through all the leaves at the outer edge of the margins. All he had to do then was to join up the prickings with lines. Sometimes the multiple lines were drawn with several pens joined together to make an instrument called a rastrum (which means rake).

Hebrew book production used a ruling frame, a wooden board with wire threaded across it. The blank sheet would have been placed on top and pressed down so that the wire impressed itself on to the sheet.

Gradual, F. Binasco, *c.* 1500–50 (New York, Pierpont Morgan Library): Adoration of the Magi.
This brilliantly coloured and minutely detailed miniature is from a Gradual, which is a book of music for Mass containing the musical parts of the Missal. All medieval churches and monasteries had a Gradual among their service books, and very many have survived.

Missal, Poitiers, late 15th cent. (Paris, Bibliothèque Nationale): Shepherds and shepherdesses dancing.
Missals, as service books used by priests to celebrate Mass, were not usually elaborately illustrated.

Opposite:
Religious treatise, France, 15th cent. (Oxford Bodleian Library): The Virgin and angels.
This full-page miniature is a companion to the manuscript on page 65 showing Christ and the angels. A heavenly host sing the praises of the Virgin Mary, accompanying themselves on stringed and keyboard instruments of many kinds. The colours are quite magnificent.

Scribes wrote with quill or reed pens, the best quills coming from a goose or swan. It would only have taken a medieval scribe a moment to prepare his quill – he would have had a great deal of practice, as the prepared point would not have lasted long before it needed recutting. There exist many contemporary pictures in medieval manuscripts of scribes at work at their desks. These show that writing was a two-handed operation – pen in one hand, knife in the other for sharpening the quill and perhaps for erasing mistakes. It would not have been difficult to scrape ink off a sheet of vellum before it had really dried. Corrections were sometimes made after the book was finished. A proof-reader would check the text and make amendments in the margin, or sometimes in the body of the text.

The scribe dipped his pen into inkwells, which were often let into the side of his desk – or he may have carried them separately if he was working out of doors. Black ink was made either from charcoal mixed with gum, or from a mixture of tannic acid with ferrous sulphate and gum added as a thickener. The most common second colour in medieval manuscripts is red, a colour which was employed from about AD 400. It was used for headings and initials (indeed headings are called 'rubrics' precisely because they were written in red), as well as

English manuscript, 15th cent. (Oxford, Bodleian Library): Warden and scholars of New College, Oxford.
Thomas Chaundler, Warden of New College 1455–75, prays with the fellows and scholars of the college. New College was founded in 1379 and this view was drawn by an anonymous artist in about 1461.

Opposite:
Religious treatise, France, 15th cent. (Oxford, Bodleian Library): Christ and the angels.
Against an intensely blue background, the angels, clad in gorgeously coloured robes – red, violet, green – have wings of many hues. They raise their hands in music and prayer to Christ, seated on a throne dappled with gold.

for lines of writing and sometimes rules as well. Its use in this way only died out with the spread of printing, when it was too complicated to print text in more than one colour.

The text from which the scribe copied (called the 'exemplar') was sometimes shown in pictures open on a table at his side, sometimes on a stand attached to his lectern. The exemplar was often held open with a weight, shown in many pictures as having a flat bottom which probably doubled as a place-marker. There must have been a considerable amount of travel to and fro with books to copy from, or scribes may have had to travel to where a book was kept in order to copy from it.

As the text was completed, perhaps several signatures or gatherings at once if more than one scribe were working on the same book, the signatures could be sent out for illustration. In order to make sure that they would later be bound in the correct order they were carefully marked on the last page of each signature with a 'catchword', that is the first word of the first page of the next signature. Sometimes the catchword was a beautiful piece of calligraphy in its own right, perhaps surrounded with flourishes and colour. With the growth of the demand for books by students of the new universities, more scribes and illuminators worked on a single book in the interests of speed, and in order to eliminate confusion new marks were introduced to indicate the number of pages within each signature. Sometimes the scribe signed his work.

The next step in the book's journey to completion was its decoration. Even before the first word was written in a book, the complete design would have been mapped out, from the overall hierarchy of design (Would there be gold throughout the manuscript? Would there be full borders on each page? Would there be full-page miniatures or only decorated initial letters?) to the design of each individual page. The rich, vibrant reds, blues and greens, the yellows and purples of the decoration were added after the text, and we can see from surviving unfinished manuscripts how spaces were roughed out in ink for the illustrations and decorated borders, or for the illuminated initials. These designs were usually copied from a pattern or from the exemplar, and could be adapted if necessary. They would have been sketched in, sometimes with guidance as to the colour to be used, before being painted. Sometimes the artist or colourist might be an itinerant professional. Experts have discerned similarities in work which indicate that in some cases artists worked as far apart as Canterbury, in northern England, and Hainault, east of London.

If gold or silver were to be used, they would be applied before any colours, because once the metal was on the page it had to be burnished, rubbed hard, and this brisk action might well damage any painting already completed. Early manuscripts have the gold applied flat to the page, gold leaf simply laid on glue and burnished when dry. In later

French manuscript, probably Simon Marmion, *c.* 1480 (New York, Pierpont Morgan Library): Annunciation to the shepherds.
The Angel Gabriel appearing to the shepherds marks the opening of the Hour of Terce. The painting is so delicate and the colours so rich and bright, that this must be by the hand of Simon Marmion of Amiens himself.

manuscripts, gold is laid on in one of two ways. In one, powdered gold is mixed with gum arabic to make a kind of gold paint, and is applied with a brush. This kind of gold was used if an animal or bird were to be painted with gold brushstrokes. For larger areas such as backgrounds, halos, or shadings, gold leaf was laid on a slightly raised ground of gesso, which gives a wonderful three-dimensional effect, like a plump golden cushion.

Gesso, the underlying material, is a mixture containing plaster of Paris, and was sometimes coloured; in Italy it was pink, in Germany brown; in Paris it was usually left white. The gesso was applied to the manuscript in a damp blob and left to dry. This work would have to have been carried out at a flat desk, unlike writing, which was often carried out at a sloping desk, because the gesso, applied wet, would have run down the page before it dried. When the gesso was completely dry, the gold leaf, cut roughly into shape, was lifted gently and smoothed into place with a scrap of silk. The gold was then rubbed with a burnishing tool, traditionally the tooth of a dog or some other carnivore attached to a handle, until it was completely smooth. The edges of the gold leaf would settle down on to the pad of gesso and the burnishing tool would nip off any surplus, which would be carefully gathered up to use again.

The rest of the decoration could now be painted. The painting may quite often have been undertaken by a different hand from that of the designer, and it is possible to see on some early manuscripts where the colours have been designated by tiny initials (probably in Latin – *azura, rubeux, viridus*): early painting by numbers. Some of the painting may have been done by pen rather than by brush, particularly the decoration on flourished initials.

Medieval manuscripts are decorated with a very wide range of colours. Vermilion is the commonest. There are other shades of red, too: madder, a plum colour, comes from the madder plant; and the exotic dragonsblood, which we are told is the mixed blood of dragons and elephants, spilt in battle (though more prosaically it actually comes from the shrub *pterocarpus draco*). Blue pigments were made from *azurite* (a blue stone rich in copper), from the seeds of the plant turnsole, from cobalt, or, most luxuriously, from *lapis lazuli*, to make ultramarine. *Lapis lazuli* comes only from the region round Afghanistan, and Marco Polo speaks of visiting the mines there at the end of the thirteenth century; but it was used in the *Lindisfarne Gospels Book* six hundred years before that, and must have been very precious for having made such a long and arduous journey. Greens were made from malachite or verdigris, yellows came from saffron or arsenic trisulphide, white from white lead. Violet was made from the sunflower.

Both the white of egg and the yolk were used to make paints of these pigments, as was animal glue made by boiling down skin and bones. Probably the illuminator bought his ingredients from an apothecary and then made up his paints for his own use, skills which were highly prized. Finally the illuminator varnished his work with gum arabic or egg white, to protect it and to make it gleam.

Professional illuminators charged for their work by the piece. In 1467 Thomas Lympnour of Bury St Edmunds charged the Paston family in England 12d each for full page illuminations; 4d each for

Livre des profits champêtres, France, 15th cent. (Paris, Bibliothèque Nationale): Grain barn. Workmen can be seen winnowing and threshing grain at the open end of a barn, well stocked for winter.

Cover of an English or Flemish Gospel Book, *c.* 1025–75 (New York, Pierpont Morgan Library): Christ and symbols of the Evangelists.

Here is an exquisite book cover from the eleventh century, gilded all over and studded with a rhythmic sequence of precious stones. A figure of Christ is set in a central oval, and at the corners are the symbols of the Evangelists. This is not simply decoration for the glory of God, but earthly treasure besides.

half-pages; 4d per hundred small painted initials, and 1d per hundred for capital letters. There is a meticulous sense of the hierarchy of decoration here, and of the relative importance of each part of the book.

When the illuminations were complete, the book was ready to be bound. The signatures were gathered carefully together in the correct order, checked over and any smudges cleaned off. Monks in the early Middle Ages would have bound their own books, probably gaining great expertise and experience over the years.

The most usual way of binding a manuscript was to stack the signatures together and then to sew them to leather thongs placed across the spine. When they were all securely held together boards were placed on either side and the thongs threaded through holes in the edge and tied or nailed down. Medieval boards were generally made of wood; oak, beech, or pine, but sometimes of leather only, or of a kind of composition board made from waste scraps glued and pressed together. Before about 1200 boards were cut flush with the edges of the pages, but later it was realized that if the edges projected slightly this would protect the pages. The edges of the pages were sometimes gilded and patterned, too, but as pages have been retrimmed over the centuries, this feature is often lost. Frequently the boards were covered with leather, sometimes dyed and stamped with patterns, but luxury books might be covered with ivory, gold or enamel, or jewels. The corners of the book were then protected with metal corner-pieces, and last of all there was usually a clasp, maybe also gold or jewelled, to keep the book closed and the pages flat.

Pictures often show books encased still further in a loose covering called a chemise, which wrapped right round the book when it was closed, and had weights in the corners so that it hung down when open in use. Books quite often had fabric covers of this kind, embroidered or perhaps of velvet. This kind of cover is now comparatively rare: textiles of course perish; and precious stones all too easily find new homes.

Parts of Germany at this time were famous for their craftsmen working in enamel and precious metals – several manuscripts produced here closely resemble metalwork (for example, the *Siegburg Lectionary*, made about 1140 at Siegburg Monastery near Cologne) in their use of tints and in the colours they chose, particularly greens and blues. By the end of the twelfth century the style was moving from the Romanesque to the Gothic, with gentler type of modelling of figures and finer more delicate brushwork.

CHAPTER 4

Other Cultures

Away from the splendour of the mainly Christian influence on illuminated manuscripts in the Western world were the evocative and moving contributions of the Jewish and Spanish cultures – rich with Eastern influence and revolutionary technique.

Overleaf:
MS Mahsor, Leipzig, *c.* 14th cent: Three Jews at prayer.
Three Jews, two wearing medieval pointed Jewish hats, stand at prayer. The faces have no nose or mouth, but only a sort of eagles's beak. It is not known why there was an artistic convention during this period to portray humans with animal faces.

Jewish

We tend to think of Judaism as having repudiated visual images and concentrated instead on its intense literary tradition. In fact, despite the biblical injunction against the making of 'any manner of likeness', there is a rich Jewish tradition of illustration and decoration of its manuscripts, as we shall see. Indeed, the ultimate source of many medieval Christian images may be very early Jewish art. During the Middle Ages, there was no fully independent Jewish artistic evolution; the illuminated books made at this time reflect the fact that Jewish communities lived within other major cultures, and their style was at all times influenced by the artistic conventions all around them. However, within these limits, Jews adapted and responded to their own religious imperatives and produced some of the finest artistic pieces to be found in the Middle Ages.

The Hebrew scribe was responsible for the whole manuscript, and sometimes for the decoration as well, and often signed his work in a colophon at the end. Hebrew script originally contained no vowels, and the text was read aloud by a vocalizer. He too often signed the manuscript. He would have been responsible for one of the most fascinating features of Hebrew manuscripts, the *masorah*. This is a commentary and notes written in the margins of the text, and often used micrography, or minute script. The writing formed the shape of all kinds of intricate geometric patterns, flowers, animals, or humans, so that when you look closely at what appears to be, perhaps, a picture of Jonah being swallowed by the whale, you see that it is composed entirely of tiny words. This practice of having the words form shapes is not found in medieval Christian art and seems to be unique to Hebrew manuscripts. The Hebrew script uses no capital letters, and the equivalent to the Christian illuminated capital letters is decorated word panels for headings. These are often works of art in their own right.

The earliest Hebrew manuscript that we know of is a book of the Prophets, made in Tiberias in Palestine in about AD 895. Interestingly, this book is a codex rather than a scroll – by contrast the Torah, the central book for Jewish worship, is still a scroll and is never illuminated. The decoration of the Tiberias manuscript echoes the style of contemporary Koran manuscripts, with abstract, geometric patterns and floral motifs, and was richly coloured and illuminated with gold. Other embellished manuscripts which have been discovered in Palestine and Egypt dating from the ninth to the twelfth century include children's textbooks, marriage contracts, and scientific books; all share the decorative tradition of Islamic manuscripts.

Spain and Portugal enjoyed a rich artistic heritage in which Islamic and mainstream Christian traditions went hand in hand. Jews thrived under the enlightened regime of Islam in the tenth and

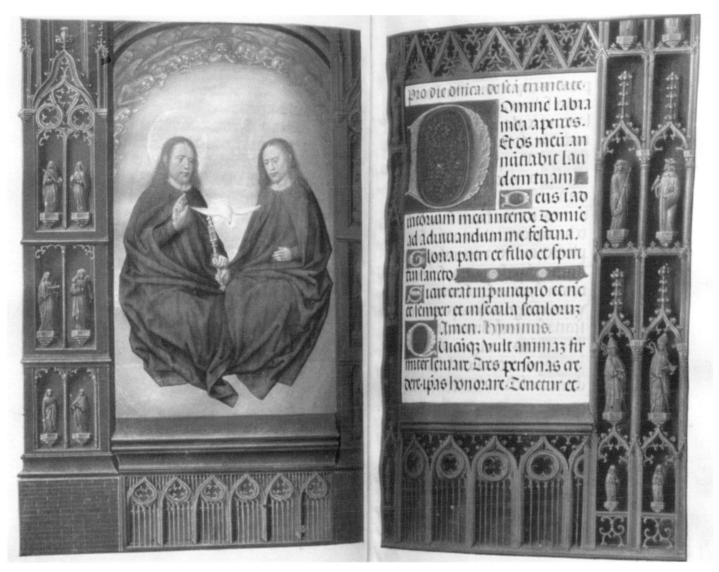

Book of Hours of Queen Isabella The Catholic, Ghent, *c.* 1492–97 (Cleveland Museum of Art): The Trinity. Isabella, Queen of Castile, married Ferdinand of Aragon in 1469, thus uniting the Spanish peninsula. In her reign both the Moors and the Jews were persecuted and driven out of Spain. This wonderful illustration shows the Trinity with the Holy Ghost in the form of a dove.

eleventh centuries, and continued to do so in Christian Spain until the fourteenth century, when Queen Isabella expelled both the Jews and the Muslims. Queen Isabella, known as The Catholic, was also responsible for introducing the feared Spanish Inquisition to keep order within the Catholic Church. Privileged and aristocratic, Jews took key positions of power under the Moors, and contemporary manuscripts are abundantly decorated. The earliest Judeo-Spanish illuminations come from such flourishing Jewish centres as Toledo and Burgos and are Bibles dating from the thirteenth century. Manuscripts from these centres were renowned for the excellence of their script and for the accuracy of their texts, and contained exquisite carpet pages – full-page illustrations dividing the main sections of the Hebrew Bible. Again the illustrative work shows the influence of Islamic decorative traditions, with complex geometric designs and entwined flowers.

While it is most unusual for a medieval Jewish artist to sign his work, in the so-called *Kennicott Bible*, made for Isaac ben Solomon de

Braga in 1476 there is a colophon in which the artist, Joseph ibn Hayyim, not only signed his name, but also used a most imaginative zoomorphic decoration of the Hebrew script, changing the plain shapes into little men and animals, fishes, birds and hares.

The other decorated Jewish book produced in numbers in Spain was the Haggadah, a collection of biblical verses, poems, and religious songs intended to be used at home during Passover. About fifteen of these manuscripts survive, mainly from the fourteenth century, and clearly show the influence of contemporary Christian art. These Haggadot parallel the popularity in Christian culture of Books of Hours, and in the same way, the pictures illustrate the text, with depictions of such events as the crossing of the Red Sea, and Daniel in the lions' den, being placed next to the very text.

We know the names of several medieval Jewish scribes and artists – one, Asher Bonnim Maymo, contracted in 1335 to copy and illuminate a Bible and two books of Maimonides for David Isaac Cohen, and Abraham ben Judah ibn Hayyim, living in Portugal in the late fifteenth century, compiled a treatise on the art of manuscript illumination.

From Ashkenazi (Franco-German) communities in the thirteenth and fourteenth centuries, we have several Bibles elaborately illustrated with pictures of events from within the text as well as with micrographic masoretic notes, the earliest having been made near Würzburg around 1233. However, the most important of these manuscript illuminations are those of the mahzor, which is a book containing the complete liturgy for holidays. These mahzorim are usually very big books and, like the enormous Bibles made in early Christian monasteries, are clearly intended for lectern use rather than for individuals. The most extensively illustrated mahzorim which survive were made in Germany: the so-called *Leipzig Mahzor* was made between 1320 and 1330, probably in the Upper Rhineland, and is painted in vivid, clear colours richly illuminated with gold. These German mahzorim contain, uniquely, pictures of human figures with animal and bird heads: but we do not know the significance of this.

Round about the end of the thirteenth century, miniatures were being painted in manuscripts in France which are almost indistinguishable from their Christian counterparts. The miniatures show such subjects as David playing his harp, or David and Goliath, and in the style of the draperies, facial expressions, and the depiction of late thirteenth-century arms and armour clearly show their Parisian models. In the fifteenth century Jewish communities were not in the ascendancy and continued to be subjected to persecution, so producing luxurious books was not a priority.

From Italy, the earliest known Jewish text is a Bible dating from around 1284 and made in Rome. From the thirteenth century onwards we start to find illuminated legal texts dealing with concepts of Jewish law and custom. Some of these texts are beautifully ornamented with framed miniatures illustrating the law in question, and with page borders of highly coloured flowers delicately twining with vines and human figures, all on a gold background. The participation of Jews, often as bankers, was central to the rise of the merchant city-states in Italy, and affluent members of the Jewish community commissioned for themselves both liturgical and secular books in the same way as the Medici or Este families were doing. Many of these books were richly decorated, with ornamental borders lavishly painted in gorgeous colours and gold leaf.

Spanish

The culture of the Iberian peninsula in the eighth century flowered in isolation from the mainstream of Europe, the territory being almost cut off by high mountains and anyway occupied in the eighth century by Muslim invaders who went on to control the peninsula for three centuries, and who contributed a rich, exotic flavour to the artistic life of the country. The manuscript illumination and script of this time are easily distinguishable as Spanish. The use of colour is quite different from mainstream Europe, and the influence of a non-Christian culture is very strong. We can see examples of this clearly in copies of the *Commentary on the Apocalypse* (better known to us, perhaps, as the Book of Revelations) composed about 776 by the monk Beatus of Liebana, of which about twenty survive. The Apocalypse was perhaps more esteemed in Spain than in other parts of Christendom; to a country riven by doctrinal difficulties, as Spain was, the book seemed to offer a guarantee of ultimate triumph over the menace to orthodoxy personified by the Muslims who occupied so much of Spain. The Spanish Church had even defined the book as a 'canonical work'. The manuscript *Commentaries* often contain miniatures which rival the text in importance, and some contain rare double-page spreads.

During the eighth and ninth centuries a rich artistic tradition took shape in north-west Spain, where more than one magnificent Bible was illuminated in this distinctively Spanish style. In the so-called *Cava Bible*, coloured inks are used on a blue-stained parchment, the writing making up the shape of a cross. The Cross was an enduring emblematic theme in the art of Spain, often used in ways not found in other parts of Europe. Other leaves in the *Cava Bible* are also purple. The Bible is now at the monastery of La Cava dei Tirreni near Naples, Italy. Another characteristically Spanish device is the labyrinth, a kind of acrostic composition which continued to be popular for centuries.

Decorations in other manuscripts also showed the influence of the Islamic culture, with ornamental adaptations of Kufic script used in

Manuscript from Asturia (detail), Spain, *c.* 950 (New York, Pierpoint Morgan Library): Noah's Ark
The white dove (shown here) on Noah's ark symbolizes the Holy Spirit, and the olive branch the Cross of Salvation. It contrasts with the black raven which represents the impure souls driven from the church.

Manuscript from Asturia, Spain, *c.* 950 (New York, Pierpont Morgan Library): Noah's Ark.

Beatus, Bishop of Liebana in Spain, who died at the end of the 8th century, was the author of several celebrated texts including a Commentary on the Apocalypse. His works were frequently illustrated over the following centuries. Although this miniature is not in good condition, the bright colours sing from the page.

illustrations, and a distinctive dot and stipple feature. It is interesting that illustrators did not try for three-dimensional images, but used colour to create flat patterns with no sense of perspective, often on backgrounds of plain coloured panels. Colours, lively and bright, take precedence over line. A Bible which was made for Abbot Maurus of the monastery of SS Mary and Martin (we are not sure where this was located) follows the tradition of the rest of Europe by opening each Gospel with an identifying author page. However, there the likeness ends. Some of the paintings use unusual circling devices as frames, and it is clear that no life model was used for the human figure. The colours are clear and vibrant and energetic, with a much greater use of yellow than that employed by artists in northern Europe.

Around the middle of the tenth century, decorated initials began to echo those which had been found in the north of France, with the same interlaced panels and knots, and it seems that Spanish scribes were beginning to be influenced not only by styles of initials but also by Carolingian models for full-page paintings. From the tenth to the eleventh centuries, what is called the Spanish Mozarabic style flourished – highly decorative, with curious border illustration and the unsophisticated liveliness of folk art. However, there was in Spain a specific archive of Biblical and Apocalyptic illustration to be found in a series of books manufactured in northern Spain between the tenth and the thirteenth centuries. Old Testament pictures copied from a Visigothic Bible can now be seen in the so-called *Leon Bible* of 960, brilliant with complex patterns and colour.

The heritage of Spain's Visigoth invaders in the fifth century persisted with what is known as 'Visigothic minuscule' handwriting, which was employed in Spanish scriptoria until the twelfth century, when a style of writing imported from France supplanted it.

Spain started to lose the distinctive character of its art under King Ferdinand I, who between 1037 and 1065 introduced new artistic themes from France. He had close ties with the great monastery at Cluny in Burgundy – indeed, Spanish gold exacted from the Muslims was to pay for a large part of the new church at Cluny at the end of the eleventh century (then, incidentally, the largest enclosed space on earth) – and his royal interests were promoted by establishing ever closer links with France, both by marriage, ecclesiastically, and politically.

Conclusion

The printing press, first used with movable type by Johann Gutenberg in Mainz in Germany in the mid-fifteenth century, signalled the end of the era of the hand-written book.

The first printers selected books to manufacture for which they felt confident they had a ready sale – it would have been expensive to produce perhaps as many as several hundred copies of a book and they would not have wanted stock to clog their warehouses. Therefore Gutenberg's first major project was, as we would expect, a Bible, the famous *Gutenberg Bible* of 1450. It was bound in two volumes, and was intended as a Lectern Bible. It was designed to look like a manuscript, and was printed with blank spaces for the illustrations, which meant that each purchaser could have his Bible decorated to suit his wishes. Other books Gutenberg produced in his very early days were Psalters, volumes of sermons, and guides to church services.

In 1465, Conrad Sweynheym and Arnold Pannartz from Germany brought the first printing press over the Alps into Italy, where the new printed books amazed and delighted the population, and eleven years later William Caxton introduced printing to Britain. It quickly became apparent that a printer could produce a book more accurately, far more quickly, and much more cheaply than a scribe and illuminator. Illustrations continued to be done by hand – indeed printers would employ their own painters, and the quality remained very high – and such texts as commemorative addresses, presentation copies, and maps were still made by hand. But the printing process was here to stay.

The new vernacular Bibles of the mid sixteenth century allowed access to the contents of the scriptures to all for the very first time – and it was now open to anyone who could read to interpret the Bible in his own way. Printed Bibles were made by the thousand – affordable, available, they changed the face of the Christian Church and with it the face of the Western world.

Opposite and above:
Medieval manuscript, Winchester Bible, 12th cent. (Winchester Cathedral): P with Elijah.
This richly ornamented initial letter is emblematic of the dedicated and highly innovative illumination techniques used in the *Winchester Bible*. The letter is a work of art in itself.

INDEX

Illuminated Manuscripts. *Book of Kells*, **8th cent.**
(Dublin, Trinity College): Opening page of St Mark's Gospel

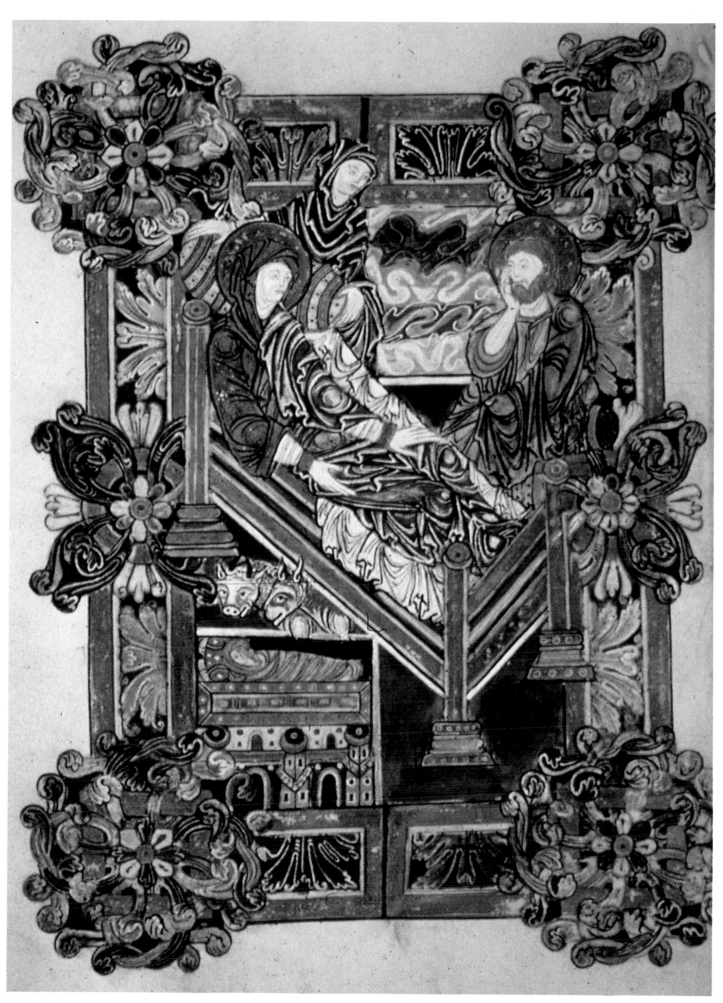

Illuminated Manuscripts. Benediction of St Aethelwold, Anglo-Saxon, *c.*975-980
(British Library): The Nativity

Illuminated Manuscripts. Psalter, Flanders, *c*.1275
(New York, Pierpont Morgan Library): St Dominic burning heretics' books

Illuminated Manuscripts. Psalter of Yolande de Soissons, Amiens, *c.*1290
(New York, Pierpont Morgan Library): St Francis preaching to the birds

Illuminated Manuscripts. *Book of Hours of Antoine de Navarre,* **15th cent.**
(Oxford, Bodleian Library): Death at home

Illuminated Manuscripts. *Book of Hours of Anne of France,* **Jean Colombe, 1480-5**
(New York, Pierpont Morgan Library): Adam and Eve

Illuminated Manuscripts. Book of Hours, Bedford Master, c.1420
(New York, Pierpont Morgan Library): Annunciation

Illuminated Manuscripts. Gradual, F. Binasco, *c.*1500-50
(New York, Pierpont Morgan Library): Adoration of the Magi